THE BOARD GAME

A Director's Companion for Winning in Business

Peter Waine

JOHN WILEY & SONS, LTD

Published in 2003 by John Wiley & Sons Ltd, The Atrium, Southern Gate,
Chichester, West Sussex PO19 8SQ, England

Telephone   (+44) 1243 779777

Email (for orders and customer service enquiries): cs-books@wiley.co.uk
Visit our Home Page on www.wileyeurope.com or www.wiley.com

Other Wiley Editorial Offices

John Wiley & Sons Inc., 111 River Street, Hoboken, NJ 07030, USA

Jossey-Bass, 989 Market Street, San Francisco, CA 94103-1741, USA

Wiley-VCH Verlag GmbH, Boschstr. 12, D-69469 Weinheim, Germany

John Wiley & Sons Australia Ltd, 33 Park Road, Milton, Queensland 4064, Australia

John Wiley & Sons (Asia) Pte Ltd, 2 Clementi Loop #02-01, Jin Xing Distripark, Singapore
129809

John Wiley & Sons Canada Ltd, 22 Worcester Road, Etobicoke, Ontario, Canada M9W 1L1

British Library Cataloguing in Publication Data

A catalogue record for this book is available from the British Library

ISBN 0-470-84764-6

Typeset in 11/16.5 pt Garamond by Footnote Graphics Ltd, Warminster, Wiltshire.
Printed and bound in Great Britain by TJ International, Padstow, Cornwall.
This book is printed on acid-free paper responsibly manufactured from sustainable forestry
in which at least two trees are planted for each one used for paper production.

CONTENTS

FOREWORD

The Board Game marks another significant milestone in the publishing partnership between the CBI and John Wiley & Sons Ltd
(Wiley). The partnership has already established a deserved reputation for delivering books which give comprehensive blueprints
for getting fast-track results across a range of key business topics.
The previous *Fast Track* series of books have been aimed squarely
at the middle management, owner-manager, consultant and trainer
markets – those involved in implementing new business techniques. *The Board Game* raises the stakes still further. Peter Waine's
insightful and entertaining book is aimed at the thought leaders of
business. It is set to become the book for company leaders, senior
and aspiring executives, and captains of industry to be seen with. It
offers an unprecedented close-up view of life at the top of the
corporate tree, and points the way to a winning formula in the
boardroom. So, I trust you will enjoy this welcome addition to our
publishing programme.

As some of you may not be fully conversant with the role of the CBI, I'd like to take a moment or two to cover our membership profile and areas of interest and responsibility. With a direct corporate membership employing over four million and a trade association membership representing over six million of the workforce, the CBI is the premier organisation speaking for companies in the UK. We represent, directly and indirectly, over 200 000 companies employing more than 40 per cent of the UK private sector workforce. The majority of blue-chip organisations and industry leaders from the FTSE 250 are members, as well as a significant number of small to medium-sized companies (SMEs)*. Our mission is to ensure that the government of the day, Whitehall, Brussels and the wider community understand the needs of British business. The CBI takes an active role in forming policies that enable UK companies to compete and prosper, and we ensure that the lines of communication between private and public leaders are always open on a national scale as well as via our regional networks. The CBI has also recently opened an office in Washington DC, in order to represent our members' interests in the US.

The appropriateness of a link between the CBI and a leading business publisher like Wiley cannot be understated. Both organisations have a vested interest in efficiently and effectively serving the needs of businesses of all sizes. Both are forward-thinkers; constantly trend-spotting to envision where the next issues and concerns lie. Both maintain a global outlook in servicing the needs of their local customers. And finally, both champion the adoption of best practice amongst the groups they represent.

I do hope you enjoy this book and would encourage you to look out for further titles from the CBI and Wiley. Here's to all the

opportunities the future holds and to success with your own
corporate agenda.

* Foreign companies that maintain registered offices in the UK are also eligible for CBI
membership.

Digby Jones
Director-General, CBI
October 2002

To

Theo and Goody

INTRODUCTION

I have taken full advantage of having access, over a decade or more, to 1000 or so main board directors, noting their opinions – usually, from their viewpoint, unwittingly! Unattributed, anonymous contributions have a certain advantage over a conventional book based on attributable sources, anecdotes and a rich array of statistics. Anecdotes can upset; they are not always the full picture and they can be personal; statistics date.

The book has an ambitious theme and is in a deliberately brief format. It is not intended as a textbook, nor as an exhaustive coverage of traditional, functional corporate themes – there are plenty of such texts available already. Nor is it a collection of corporate homilies. Rather, the goal is to attempt to encapsulate and make some sense of the criteria which a plethora of directors believe, very sincerely, to be the most important lessons learned as viewed from a varied and senior perspective. Where possible, the text has been supplemented by direct experience.

Peculiarly and unexpectedly, a number of impressions have emerged. First and foremost, what is regarded as utterly perceptive and clearly of real value to successful directors appears on paper to be almost obvious, modest and mundane. Second, unlike conventional business books, where one book can give the ten tablets of stone on how to be an effective marketing or finance director or whatever, and then another promptly contradicts the first – and yet there are directors who are equally successful by adopting either sets of values – this book approaches business from an altogether different viewpoint. Interestingly, there is a remarkable consensus between directors when viewing corporate life as a generalist, rather than as a functional head.

It is primarily a view from the board, hopefully relevant to those who have already reached that level but equally to those who aspire to. Perhaps, it also has merits and relevance to those who may want to have a peep at what actually goes on around the board table and into the minds of the directors themselves, even if they never personally aspire to join those ranks. Maybe it will encourage some to view matters differently and help others to understand better what they should be looking for.

Certain themes and conclusions link the otherwise disparate elements of this review of the workings of businesses, regardless of their size and status. It is difficult to avoid the assumptions that running commercial organisations is relatively easy, that it is an exercise made to appear rather difficult by those at the top, and that the line between relative success and failure is a narrow one.

Furthermore, people and what is done for and with them are the ultimate cornerstone of the building blocks for a successful company. However strong the other factors – such as strategy, appropriate structures, the ability to change and make change permanent – people remain the pivotal element.

Then there are the undeniable facts that some directors are more lucky than able, that others will not repeat their initial successes and that too many still are not encouraged to make mistakes and learn from them or are not given sufficient time at the top in order to succeed.

Despite its international status and relative success, the City is not on the whole either liked or admired by those on the boards of commercial companies; the old bogey of City short-termism, with its constant pressure to make another deal or deliver performances at the expense of the longer term, persists. There is also an unhealthy probity gap between the City with its power and agenda (with its own relatively poorly managed financial service companies), and its generally better managed clients. Consequently, there is an inability on behalf of the City to recognise and invest in good management. The City on the whole is not a welcomed partner, but rather a cruel necessity.

And then there is the regressive matter of under-utilising half of the potential labour force – women – and why few women have reached the top and whether this situation will change and over what likely period. The assumption here is clearly that the so-called glass ceiling will be smashed and sooner than most anticipate.

As for the ability of firms to trade outside their national borders, whether within the rest of the EU or internationally, most find such opportunities irresistible. Yet the majority of their endeavours end in disappointment or partial failure, and large sums of money and time meanwhile will have been expended and reputations dented or destroyed.

Smaller companies and private ones, so often dismissed as the havens of mediocrity or, in the case of the latter, even the butt of comedians, are in practice stronger vehicles for economic growth or havens for entrepreneurs than their larger brethren.

Neither takeovers, mergers nor joint ventures are the quick fix or shortest route to riches and glory – despite their apparent lure and attraction. CEOs – pressed by the City and with temperaments ripe for constant activity – find such corporate excesses persuasive. As in the case with trading outside the United Kingdom, so here too; many ventures end in disappointment, more in relative failure. Yet no company can afford to remain static, stating that they have reached the position they seek and intend to remain there. Companies evolve and the competition does not stand still.

It is a foolish board which ignores its own culture or neglects the fact that people and organisations do not necessarily operate to the same timescales. Get one out of kilter with the other – the wrong appointment or the wrong pace of change – and trouble will not be long in coming.

Many of the keys to corporate success lie in timing and balance – when to act, or merely think, how much data is necessary before taking the plunge. Unfortunately, IT is a mixed blessing; it can give directors access to excessive data, restricting them from seeing the general themes, the critical overall view.

Other keys are relationships between board members and with those below, and between the company and its customers and the shareholders. The ultimate relationship is that between the chairman and CEO – one which needs to be clearly defined and based on mutual respect and appropriate chemistry. The chairman runs the board, the CEO the company, and the decisive role of the chairman is to sack the CEO. The final role of the non-executive directors (NEDs), with the chairman at their head, is to take the reigns in difficult and awkward times.

The ambivalent effect of sentiment is also discussed, how it can bind longer-term relationships or prevent directors making the right decisions.

Corporate governance is given a good airing. It warrants it. Some companies still do not wholeheartedly believe in it; others are attempting to make it an industry in itself; many more, fortunately, are embracing the tool both realistically and relevantly for them. The NED should not second-guess the executives, but must, in turn, be truly independent – both psychologically and financially – and act as both a confidant and mentor, without forgetting to be courageous and curious as well. While acting sometimes as a voice of caution they must never be a policeman, merely ticking the corporate boxes. The NED is there to ensure that the CEO dreams, but realistically; and implements policies, but only after due diligence. So the role of NEDs is positive. They are the outsiders with an insider feel, whose remuneration should be fair but not excessive and never too great to curtail their independence. The greatest advantage accruing to the NED is not directly financial; it is a question of going to teach and coming away learning.

In a company, the challenge and the sheer pace of corporate life make business one of the basic yet most absorbing of all human activities. Hopefully this speedy tour of that scene will encourage some, stimulate others and rouse the curiosity of the rest, however divorced they may erroneously believe their chosen lifestyle to be from a healthy economy. In the process, perhaps some will avoid preventable mistakes.

Lastly, a thank you to Cherry Caselton who typed and frequently retyped every chapter. As with a speech, the shorter it is the harder is its composition; made even more of a challenge when attempting a subject so wide and important as that of commercial gain via human endeavour.

Peter Waine
Digswell Place
October 2002

1
THE CHAIRMAN AND THE CEO

The relationship between the chairman and his CEO is *the* relationship in corporate life. There is no other that can compare and the consequences of failure are wide, deep and comprehensive. Yet, in essence, there are really only two factors to bear in mind – chemistry and an understanding between the two as to what their respective roles are within the board and corporate structure.

Surprisingly, the final ascent to either position is similar, despite the two roles being so very different. It is often rather unstructured or left to luck. Some go straight from executive director to chairman, others via being CEO; the former can lead to a chairmanship of his own board, the latter hardly ever.

As a spectator of the corporate scene, reflecting on corporate failures, it is too easy to conclude that the odds against a successful relationship are legion and the corresponding chances of success minimal. There may be a subtle overlay of various factors which can all too easily create instant havoc, either in isolation or combined, but even these do not constitute a bolt out of the blue. They are usually slow to germinate and give all concerned ample notice of their pending arrival; that is, if anybody bothers to watch for them and knows from whence they might come.

It is always fun, albeit somewhat cheeky, to engage either the chairman or CEO in conversation, in isolation talking about the other. Usually, the more fascinating discourse is the CEO commenting on his chairman. What appears to many, even to those closely involved, to be a happy, workable, meaningful relationship is actually nothing of the sort. What the eye sees is not what the heart feels.

Why should this be? Surely both or either are perceptive and mature enough to know if all is not what it seems, or do something practical to resolve the matter? Alas, the answer is "Yes and No" – "Yes" that both realise the reality, but "No" they cannot easily do much about it, at least in the short term.

WHY IT CAN ALL GO WRONG

Company politics play a destructive and ugly part. A CEO might have a chairman forced upon him by history – inherited from the past, or imposed by the detail of an agreed merger or takeover. One company gets the chairman slot, the other that of CEO. Or again either of them joins with a CV to die for but doesn't perform to plan.

Other reasons for it going wrong are not difficult to pinpoint. Perhaps the chairman or CEO were lucky last time around and their luck has now run out; the same factors have not combined again. Alternatively, with success comes complacency. A person can only eat so many meals in a day, wear so many clothes. One of them is no longer sufficiently hungry. Deep down, he might have taken the position, especially if it is the chairmanship, primarily for status or for money. If the chairman, he could even disguise reality for some time, especially if the CEO does not know what an effective chairman can contribute and therefore he does not know what he is missing. The company is doing the chairman a favour; the chairman is not doing the company one. (Both chairmen and CEOs can land each other in deep water, if either shirks from facing problems. To deny the existence of a problem is common in business life, even if the problems themselves vary. Yet they do not vary as much as many believe!)

In these circumstances, both or either, in league or separately, believe that by ignoring a problem it will go away. It will not; it will merely get worse. The remedy is to communicate the problem early and not to be afraid. This is especially a problem with smaller companies where the chairman or CEO feels more possessive towards "his" company and does not want to think that anything could be wrong – he is almost too proud to confess. When in crisis the chairman needs to calm everything and everybody down, try to pull people back from acting rashly, ask the question, "What are the real issues, not the perceived one?" The board collectively needs to stop, take a deep breath, see what can be done. Otherwise, everyone wants to be a hero; some are even prepared to lay down their life for the challenge at hand. If the chairman panics, the tone is set, the board freezes, the company goes into a corporate nosedive. Nobody can do anything.

There is more than one scenario of the board in crisis. Is it due to the company doing badly or the CEO underperforming? The two can be directly linked, but are not necessarily so. If the former, then the chairman – again – will need to be proactive and mobilise his non-executive directors (NEDs). If the latter, then it is an operational crisis, and it is for the CEO to resolve the problem with the NEDs' backing. In neither case panic; but do not delay too long either.

When a board splits, another variation of the crisis manifests itself. Fortunately, for some at least, certain boards are more susceptible to splits than are others. Boards which are relatively new, or which have not been together for very long, tend to suffer from "my speciality" syndrome. Do not tread on my territory or contest my authority in my functional area. Taking a board into a broader constituency will be regarded by one director as a personal challenge!

Also prone to splits are boards composed of directors with a wealth of experience – the "not invented here" syndrome. "Do not try it, it will not work." Such boards are usually old established ones who cannot see beyond the immediate and are therefore closed to new ideas.

Even an NED can create a split, if he has a bee in his bonnet. He might believe that cash is king, having presided over a cash mountain, but he forgets that a cash mountain may be more of an asset when interest rates are historically high but is not when they are historically low. Getting him to let the company spend it in order to invest can be a tortuous and tedious exercise.

Boards can panic when there is a hostile bid. Once in the fray, the board will probably believe its own propaganda and publicity. Yet the bidder will neatly counter-argue that if it was that simple for the board, why did it not act accordingly before?

If a board is successful in fighting off a hostile bid, the problems are not over. How then does it execute promises made in the heat of battle? With victory comes the awful realisation that it was probably only a hollow one. Few make hostile bids on a whim. Rather there is value to be extracted via a brand, synergy, etc. If the win is followed by terminal pain, it would have been better to have lost. And remember, most hostile bids are won in the first 24 hours.

THE FUNDAMENTALS TO LOOK OUT FOR

There is little that can be done in respect of chemistry except, of course, to acknowledge its existence. As a minimum, mutual respect between the chairman and the CEO can be fostered and a co-operative relationship established. But that is the limit of any such exercise. The rest is chemistry. In most cases, two people are aware if the chemistry is right or wrong and probably at their first meeting. It is neither's fault if the chemistry is wrong; it is both their faults if they are aware of it and ignore the incompatibility. The right chemistry is a cement between them, a reason for working together, the joined-up element of corporate governance especially when the going gets tough. And often the corporate path is a rough and rocky challenge. Even conventionally run companies, usually the larger ones or those who dominate their niche markets, may be merely enjoying a fool's comfort just before the storm. Or the end of conventional, routine corporate affairs may be self-inflicted or even planned.

The cuckoo in the nest is the acquisition, or the takeover, the merger or the joint venture which is ill-conceived, unchallenged or pursued with rose-tinted glasses. The company digests a large mouthful, the cultures are different; either one or the other, or neither, prevails, and the company is in trouble. Meanwhile, the company expends and often wastes a great deal of time and effort taking its eye off its core activities and acting disloyally toward its agreed strategy.

There is even a case to be made for saying that a company's reputation is also one of its principal assets and therefore that decisions can, and probably will, damage the reputation of the organisation. Few worry at the time; the City has probably advocated it, the chairman is too weak to stop his CEO and the latter can see only the upside. Either way, one fact is clear. At the helm will be the chairman and the CEO, dangerously exposed, often lonely, in need of a relationship which is, at least, both meaningful and mutually respected. It leaves the chairman exposed, operating in the glare of the open market, needing to make major decisions quickly and often at the expense of current corporate culture.

As for the second reason for failure – a lack of understanding between the two as to what are their respective roles – an entire book could be written on this alone. Yet there are few that address it, even fewer that give the subject either thought or reflection.

THE BOARD IN CRISIS

Boards in crisis often simply do not realise that that is the state they are in. The malaise and the symptoms might not show quickly; the executive team might be scared to open up as this could result in a loss of face or lead to an accusation of undermining colleagues. The board becomes toothless.

Companies respond best in a crisis when their boards are smaller, and when the executive team recognises quickly, albeit retrospectively, that radical action needs to be taken. If the executives are heavily and emotionally involved – perhaps some of them helped create the company in its present guise and hold considerable equity, or the company is owner-driven – then the chances of success can be enhanced. They have a vested interest, a lean and hungry commitment. Otherwise, it is left more to the NEDs to take the lead. Often it is down to one person – the CEO – and his relationship with the chairman.

If the CEO is a strong personality, committed to the business, he is more likely to take the medicine compared with the journeyman appointed as part of a longer career. And to get the turnaround in time, the CEO, the board, the shareholders, all need their share of old-fashioned luck!

TWO ROLES, DIFFERENT ATTRIBUTES

The chairman's role is to run the board and that of the CEO to run the company. A simple statement, but not oversimplistic. The two roles, while they should be complementary, are different and require different skills. A chairman needs to possess well-honed sensitivities, to be a good listener and mentor, to be a person who can encourage debate at the expense of presentation and be aware that the buck stops ultimately with him. He needs to be conscious of the shareholders' interests. It is a rather ethereal role, but none the worse for that, not inferior to the practical, high-profile CEO role, and no sinecure. It demands different skills from any acquired prior to the actual appointment. A chairman adopts a role for which he has no recognisable apprenticeship.

Some boards appoint an external candidate straight to the chairmanship. That conveys different messages to different audiences – the City, employees, fellow directors and the media. It usually means that the succession has not been planned.

There is nothing wrong in recruiting new talent from outside – indeed it is often right. Existing teams can become complacent, comparing their performance with internally set yardsticks and forgetting that the competition outside does not stand still. But the way forward is to recruit the chairman as chairman designate, making him a non-executive director from whence he emerges – possibly within only 12 months and by the next AGM or even sooner (heirs apparent tend not to be patient people!).

The CEO, on the other hand, will be an altogether different person, no shrinking violet, a person who needs his ego constantly massaged, to be given credit even when credit is not due, encouraged and yet channelled, stimulated and yet remaining a corporate realist. Ultimately, the role of the chairman is to dismiss the CEO. (Of course, while all CEOs need their egos massaged, the degree varies greatly. The amount will depend upon his own self-confidence; his length of time at the top, possibly as a CEO; his knowledge of other companies and sectors and his respect for the real or perceived strengths of his chairman – and those of the rest of the board.)

THE CHAIRMAN'S SKILL SET

The best chairmen share a group of skills; the worst are there for the easy ride, for the status, the money, the excuse to put a tie on and leave the house as they did when they were executive directors (to the relief of their spouses who have their own independent lives and covet their freedom – a chairmanship can save a marriage).

A chairmanship is executive or non-executive, potentially full time or virtually being a figurehead. A good corporate game is to telephone a company and ask the receptionist for the name of the chairman. Most do not know; most cannot name their head. Does that mean that the chairman is more figurehead than the ultimate repository of all executive and non-executive power? No, but his power is often on loan to his fellow board colleagues, except at board meetings themselves; his executive powers are a gauntlet to be grasped when circumstances dictate. Nobody else is qualified to fulfil that role.

Similar, incidentally, is the case of the role of the chairman's wife – if she is not the company's hostess nobody else can play that role either. A vacuum will be left – yet most chairmen's wives are kept out of the corporate equation. Many do not even know the rudimentary economics of their husband's company. This is not being condescending, but practical. Somebody needs, on occasion, to be the company's hostess, a contribution which is beyond and in addition to the efforts of professional PR firms. It is also necessary for the chairman's wife to be aware of the company's character and performance. What goes on in the corporate world overspills into the private and vice versa.

The best chairmen understand the City, a knowledge acquired either by being on the board of a commercial company that has operated closely with the Square Mile or, as second-best, via a career in financial services. Second-best because while the City attracts able individuals it is not renowned for the way it runs its own firms. Those in financial services tend to be observers of the corporate scene, in the gallery watching, or involving themselves where they have bought the right to do so or have the power to influence, but they are not the corporate world's best managers.

The best chairmen lead but are also part of their teams. They need to be nimble, occasionally vacating the chairman's chair, joining in the debate but knowing when to don the mantle again. They are not one of the lads; only sometimes are they temporary and honorary ones. It is a challenge and an opportunity offered to no other corporate player. They are a corporate hybrid.

The chairman should understand how lonely it is being a CEO, hence the need for him to be an effective confidant and mentor. The CEO is around when the chairman has gone home; alone with his executive colleagues, all of whom have careers of their own, reputations to build on, company politics to play and the sheer basic human instinct to survive.

Oddly, the chairman can be too close to the CEO to be a truly effective confidant and mentor! And yet it is one of his prime responsibilities. There is a need for the chairman to become, not the father of the growing prodigy, but his godfather – the outsider with the insider feel, with a genuine affection for his CEO and a wish to see him succeed.

In turn, he needs to be prepared to give his CEO the limelight and, as already said, the credit as well. And as youth has optimism and confidence, so the best CEOs have entrepreneurialism and energy – but these need to be controlled, harnessed and developed. The corporate godfather, better known as an effective chairman, plays that role.

Indeed, the chairman should avoid offering executive direction. He can propose ideas, privately or indirectly, in the hope that the point will be taken at the right moment; in normal times, no more and no less.

It is important from the psychological perspective for the chairman not to have an office in the same building as his CEO. Having no office helps to show to all, especially to the CEO, that the latter does, in reality, run the company on a day-to-day basis. It is his show. There is then no temptation for either to drop in too frequently to the other's office, making the relationship too restrictive and claustrophobic.

There has been a long and fashionable debate over whether a chairman is executive or non-executive. He is both; inclining towards one or other depending upon the situation. Ultimately, he must also be independent; perhaps owning sufficient equity to be motivated, but not too much to be bought, having no secret agenda and being beholden to no one either in the company or outside. "Sufficient" here means no more than single figure percentages of the total equity in the company, possibly with a ceiling of under 5 per cent. (There can, and inevitably will, be a breach of this ceiling when the chairman has bought into a younger company or when joining around the time of a float, as part of a package. But that is a way of offering incentive and motivation in a company with either a poor or non-existent track record or where the company, still small, is attempting a massive change in corporate identity.)

To highlight the singular attributes of the chairman is not to isolate him. He cannot thrive on his own. He needs a dynamic relationship between himself and his CEO.

THE CHAIRMAN AND HIS CEO: THE DYNAMICS

The most effective chairmen and CEOs keep their eye on today's issues while concurrently seeking to interpret what is happening on the horizon – a difficult balance but a required one, nonetheless. The great companies are in control, they pre-empt events whenever or wherever possible. The chances of achieving this are greatly enhanced if the NEDs, led by their chairman, understand the difference between being executive and non-executive; then they can see the wood for the trees. They are like a helicopter pilot, hovering over the scene, taking it all in.

In the good times – those conventional moments when the company seems to be in control of its own destiny; when external factors, whether international, governmental or sector-based, are not all-intrusive – then the chairman is primarily non-executive. When the unexpected happens, which is usually at least partly predictable in retrospect – when the company is active with takeovers and the like – then the chairman becomes more executive.

When times are dire and the corporate doors are being rattled, the chairman is the lonely sailor on the deck wondering why on earth he ever took on the job in the first place. It becomes about as entertaining as a Gothic novel. His reputation is on the line; failure will stick persistently to his CV. To say that it would have been worse had he not been in charge does not satisfy either the head-hunter or the City.

No wonder few CEOs can, or should, become chairman of another company. They would not have the time to run one company as a chairman and the other as a CEO especially in the difficult times when both roles are equally executive. Furthermore, if one person combines both roles – not with the same company, but in two separate ones – he will be judged ultimately and most immediately by the shareholders and analysts, staff and colleagues of the company at which he is the CEO.

By the way, NEDs should be aware that a chairman and CEO working in unison, if they choose to keep their NEDs in the dark, can almost always achieve this. And not only is the average directors' and officers' liability cover inadequate, but even an adequate one cannot cover for loss of reputation. Increasingly, the potential liability of being a director is becoming prohibitive, with the adverse consequences visiting those of the next generation!

There are some directors who have handed over all their assets –
apart from their golf clubs – to their spouses! And yet there is an
obvious need to be positive.

In the good times, it is fun to be chairman. He is almost a
figurehead. At other times he is in charge, the buck stops squarely
with him, and it can be hell or the chance to prove his mettle, his
true worth; the opportunity to enhance a corporate reputation.
(Interestingly, some chairmen make poor NEDs on other boards;
they are used to being obeyed, even if their authority is admin-
istered subtly. They cannot always slip effortlessly or naturally into
the discussion mould.)

Can one person combine the two roles in the same company?
Until the recent spate of corporate governance reports, starting with
Cadbury and so far finishing with Turnbull, the answer was: "Yes,
perhaps". But because the skills are different, it is like making a
person both head of state and head of government. If the roles are
split then great caution must be shown over which of the two roles
the present incumbent chooses. There are examples, all too frequent, where the wrong choice has been made and the company
and share price have suffered. In turn, some have regarded that
debacle as ammunition against the corporate governance industry.
That is unfair; only the consultants or those frightened of effective
corporate governance argue thus. It is merely a question of bad
management, nothing more nor less.

Surprisingly, and pleasantly so, many chairmen, even those who
are otherwise rather inept or superficial, can excel under pressure;
cometh the hour cometh the man. After the storm, they either slip
effortlessly back into their traditional mould or, more usually,
decide that they have had enough, have done their duty, and look
for their successor; in the meantime, surprising everybody except

perhaps themselves. When he re-emerges the company might also have, or be recruiting, a different CEO.

It is crucial at board meetings for the chairman to invite all to speak, seek judgements and opinions, and encourage all to say what they really think. It is an art, a corporate skill; after the board meeting, his executive colleagues will have to re-establish their workable, everyday relationships. What has been said cannot be unsaid and memories can be long. (It is not unheard of for a former colleague to be named as a referee, perhaps when the former is seeking an NED position, believing him to be a safe referee, only to find that the reference is less than good and it scuppers his NED prospects. Nothing too specific; merely a pause or a subtle, virtual reality, knowing wink, but sufficient to do the damage.)

The reason for this unexpected behaviour is the fact that the chairman or CEO will have beaten a number of people to reach those august levels and, by so doing, will also have created people who could, and sometimes do, harbour a grudge. Asking that source to be a referee is a golden, long-awaited opportunity to balance the corporate books. Silly, almost juvenile, but fact.

There may be occasions when it is useful for the chairman to resort to a secret ballot. This can be a strange and difficult precedent but conceivably a useful executive tool to have up the sleeve. The main point, however, is to ensure that real debate takes place, that no recrimination follows and that the team goes forward as a team after the board meeting has finished.

One of the persistent and growing challenges to board effectiveness is the modern desire for data; facts regardless of their real relevance. It is a direct consequence of an IT-orientated society which, in turn, means that directors increasingly possess more and more facts and yet rely even more on others for the complete picture. The directors take the problem with them into the board-room. They should leave it outside.

This propensity is found at any stage, level or size of company. That is why so many takeovers, mergers and joint ventures disappoint. Many of them cannot be accused of having insufficient data prior to signing the original agreements. This itch is seen during routine board meetings. Finance directors present a ream of figures which can easily, either intentionally or not, confuse and hinder the trends, the very facts on which a main board needs to concentrate. It takes a little coaxing and persuasion to retrain a finance director into letting go, offering only a selection of data. This is especially so in the case of conglomerates or with companies which have many subsidiaries, and perhaps spread internationally. Younger directors are also prone to succumbing to a superabundance of IT-generated data due to their lack of practical experience, as too are companies with weak and ineffectual NEDs.

The board is not the executive committee, it is the policy-making forum. The chairman needs to be acutely aware of this and encourage a relevant boardroom attitude.

A good combination, and a perfect balance, is to have an intuitive chairman, an ambitious but listening chief executive, and a finance director who is especially good with figures and details. (It is a corporate impossibility to be effective either as a chairman or as a CEO and be financially illiterate.)

It is worth remembering, especially at this level, that the line between success and failure can be breathtakingly narrow, the difference between one person, an external factor or sheer bad luck.

There is an art, viewed by both the company and the individual, of turning a mistake into a positive advantage, a weakness into a strength. Not enough directors and, of course others, are paid to make a mistake, but from mistakes can come real insight, strength and gain. For the larger company there may be room for some failures; alas, not so for the smaller ones. They have less leeway, less fat, less to fall back on. It is fundamental, therefore, that the chairman acknowledges that possibly fewer than half of the board decisions will be right. He will need to develop a culture of curiosity, rewarding courage and lateral thinking and yet leading a board which, when it is time for action, will hand the executive baton to the CEO.

Both the chairman and the CEO will find the chances of establishing a meaningful relationship much easier, and positive, if they understand each other's different roles. And the variety of combinations of factors which will influence each other is legion. For instance, when the CEO is an entrepreneur – creating a company, dominating his local scene, uncomfortable with the larger organisation, used to being proved right against the odds – additional skills are required by the chairman. The latter will need to channel that entrepreneurialism without stifling it, introduce more systems but only the right amount – not too little, too late, or too much, too soon. The conventional structure will be a cruel necessity, and hopefully acceptable, because it is the chairman, with the right chemistry, advocating it. The circle is completed.

THE CEO: NO SHRINKING VIOLET

Nor should a CEO be judged on the immediate performance of the company. A newly floated entity, for example, is almost bound to do well initially – everything was geared for a successful float. It is the CEO – who is there before and after the float, who produces sustained performance for each of the next two or three years and, in the meantime, creates a culture appropriate to the evolving corporate entity – who deserves the credit. And the ultimate credit for that achievement goes to the chairman; it is he who should ensure that the corporate pieces, the building blocks, are in place. He will help to make change permanent.

Some of the best CEOs are those who offer energy and excitement in their deliberations; they speak the language that says that their company has a corporate statement which offers clarity of purpose, ensures that all colleagues understand the perceived corporate goals and have a sense of owning them. The CEO will then release the energy to achieve those results. It can be an exciting ride for all concerned, not least for the CEO and his chairman – a deeply satisfying experience.

Speed is crucial. On being appointed, especially as CEO, there is the equivalent of the political 100 days, setting out your stall, your approach, but avoiding detail and hostages to fortune. One of the "musts" for that finite period is to get rid of certain people before you know them personally and before colleagues say, "A bit late doing that". Interestingly, and reassuringly, most who are asked to leave will agree with you in due course, so do not be too weak or feel too much of a brute.

(Some issues only become board ones when there has been failure at a lower level. Risk is a line function, along with safety, but if either goes wrong, it readily becomes a board problem. It is wise when below the board, but aspiring to reach it, never to surprise a main board. Make sure the information flow is good. The nature of business is to take risk, but it is also to assess the right degree of risk for that company; the acceptable threshold will vary from company to company.)

Crucially, the CEO should not have many biases when it comes to function. Whereas previously he will have headed a function and thus come via a particular route to the main board, it is important that, as CEO, he understands that he is now a main board generalist attempting impartially to balance the views of all, rather than being biased towards any one function, department or division.

A CEO, however ambitious, young or energetic, can have only two or three ideas to mull over in his mind simultaneously if he is to remain sufficiently focussed. That is not an excuse for the chairman to discourage the CEO from having visions and dreaming dreams. Too often CEOs become cynical and dream too infrequently (or they do not have minds that are open to outcomes, but only to inputs). The trick is the putting of substance to those dreams and evaluating the aspirations behind them, and it is the role of the chairman to do just that. At times he will be proactive and at other moments will act in response to the CEO. A sensitive and subtle approach needs to be adopted by all concerned. It is easy to be a wishful thinker when you want to get something done, and it is necessary to believe in order to achieve. But if there is no realistic check the company can regress into deep trouble.

It is unwise for a CEO to trust the professionals with anything. If something does go wrong he will have no redress. He will be friendless and isolated. Better to trust his instincts and his colleagues, while listening to a broader church.

WHEN THINGS START TO GO WRONG

Where the chairman originally appointed the CEO, there is a special relationship between the two. The chairman will want to make the relationship work in a very special way – almost, but not quite, regardless – and thereby vindicate his original appointment. It can lead to undue, unhelpful cosiness or to a bond, cemented by chemistry. If the chairman is appointed after the CEO, it is rather different. The CEO will feel more reassured – he would have played a crucial part in the selection – but that should not mean greater comfort, merely a better chance of the relationship working.

Obviously, it is not wise to change the chairman and chief executive at the same time, nor even within a short period of each other. Because strong boards are in control of events they will be in control of the timing of the two appointments. Furthermore, by appointing them at different times, it is possible to tweak the specification to accommodate the strengths and weaknesses of the other incumbent. The board is not then working in a vacuum or with a hypothetical model.

One of the greatest skills demanded of a CEO is the ability to brief the City effectively. This will be developed specifically in Chapter 3. Here we need only touch briefly on a simple truth. Many high-fliers are not exposed to the Square Mile prior to joining the board and there are a number of main board directors who have no direct familiarity with the City prior to becoming CEO. The CEO can become overwhelmed by the mystique of the City; a mystique based on ignorance, not fact. Some CEOs will claim that they do have prior experience, but often it is merely a question of briefing colleagues who then brief the analysts.

CONTROLLING AND ENHANCING THE CEO

As so much is expected of a CEO, it is *ipso facto* imperative to motivate him and retain his services. There is a world of difference, however, between being bullied, overpaying or underpaying him (all will demotivate in practice – the second stopping him being hungry, the last making him feel dissatisfied, his services acquired on the cheap). Getting the balance right is crucial. The problem can be complex and compounded – for instance, how to prevent a CEO getting what he demands if he does not deserve it and yet knows he can get it elsewhere. The tantrum scenario of the CEO who appears to have most of the trump cards, at least in the shorter term, is exhausting for the chairman and yet will quickly become his priority. Alas, again, there are examples of weak chairmen, undermined by equally weak remuneration committees, the latter the Achilles' heel of modern corporate life. Nonsenses are propounded and perpetuated, consolidated and made to look legitimate, in the name of the deliberations of remuneration committees. The best boards encourage the CEO to do things outside the minimum but clearly defined, and then recognise and compensate accordingly – no more, no less.

While some chairmen do too much, some do too little and others perform unexpectedly well in times of trouble. Successful boards are examples of balance – between competing interests, personalities, functions, internal/external factors, good and bad luck, and a legion of other apparently incompatible or demanding issues. Ultimately, the key to success is the relationship between the chairman and his CEO. In practice, boards often make a difficult challenge more difficult or impossible. It need not be so.

2
CORPORATE GOVERNANCE

There is a chance that consultants will make corporate governance a new and lucrative industry for them at the expense of
the benefits which a properly regulated governance debate could
offer. The fear is further compounded by the existence of relatively
little evidence of any correlation between an effectively composed
board of NEDs, and a better bottom line. And yet the City
institutions are on the whole supportive of more professionally
appointed NEDs, believing that it is both logical and common sense
that a link and correlation does exist, and realising, in turn, that
NEDs are the catalyst at board level for effective corporate
governance. They will be both the tutors and the eyes and ears of
their executive colleagues.

The concept of NEDs is still rather misunderstood; they are seen
possibly as jobs for the boys, cosy corporate relationships, recip-
rocation of favours with positions on each other's boards, a

retirement job, or jobs for the great and the good at the exclusion of all others.

THE BENEFITS TO THE COMPANY

Fortunately, apart from a few isolated instances, that scenario is totally outdated. The best NEDs are excellent value for money, costing less than a PA (no National Insurance Contribution, a relatively small director's fee – no salary as they are not technically employees). They provide an outside view, remaining the outsider yet aware of the tensions and relationships, the art of the possible and the aspirations and fears of their executive colleagues – or they should do.

In the process they can "control" the chairman who in turn "controls" the CEO, who, as observed in Chapter 1, runs the company. The NED is a central link in the business-to-boardroom chain.

Furthermore, he can offer an international and/or EU perspective, more important than many might realise. He can act as a restraining influence if the company believes that the rest of the EU or the world is a place where the grass is greener. In difficult times, the NED will come into his own, just as the leader of the NED team – the chairman – will do as well. He is more likely to see the wider perspective having a more detached viewpoint, to be less personally involved and consequently to offer a balanced, unfussy and cooler deliberation. Unlike his executive colleagues, he has no career in the company, other than possibly becoming chairman.

On a constant basis, the NED will also help to improve and refine board processes and procedures. The appointing of an NED can reflect the changing needs of a company more easily than changing the executive directors and yet can also offer continuity if an executive director resigns or is dismissed.

There are times when the NED will be easily the most appropriate director to maintain an ethical climate on the board – a difficult role and one requiring courage. Indeed, the best NEDs stand out because they do demonstrate courage – along with curiosity. Again, it is partly because they are neither executive nor do they have a career in the company.

The best NEDs are not policemen, ticking boxes, merely ensuring that nobody breaks the corporate governance rules. They have a much wider, more exciting and positive contribution than that. Certainly, there was every prospect that they might develop along those negative, unexciting ways because the original idea of the corporate governance reports emanated from the Stock Exchange. Sir Adrian Cadbury, the chairman of the first such report, deserves much credit merely for setting a pace and cultural background that have allowed the debate to develop, while at the same time not being sidetracked or hijacked by those who have a vested interest in seeing it all fail.

NEDs can act as confidants and mentors to the chairman and to other members of the board, an especially rewarding role if an NED adopts a younger or more recently appointed executive board member, reassuring him that the recession is not the first such recession, that there can and should be a bright new dawn awaiting. Again, a question of encouraging the wider, less introverted corporate perspective.

To have the scope and the platform, let alone the expectation and the right corporate culture, an NED needs to be appointed first and foremost as a generalist and not, therefore, to rectify some technical imbalance on the board. If the company has such a problem it should make the necessary executive appointment. The NED should not be curtailed in that way. Sometimes it is rather difficult to avoid it, however, especially in smaller firms. In the latter, it might be a question, for instance, of the finance director really being a financial controller masquerading as a finance director, getting left behind as the company grows. Cunningly, but wrongly, the board hope that an NED who is a finance director can fill this executive skills gap. He cannot and nor should he be tempted.

The NED should be allowed and encouraged to contribute widely, even on matters in which he is not an expert. His naive question can be just the one that others wished they had asked, but did not have the courage to do so.

GETTING THE BEST OUT OF NEDs

In order to carry out his responsibilities effectively, assuming that he knows what they are in the first place, the NED needs to be truly independent. After all, that is possibly a truer, more disciplined title for the position even if it is one which, despite the efforts of some, is not and will not replace that of NED. To be "independent", the director should not be related to any senior member of staff, and not necessarily be known personally prior to the appointment. He should be selected via open competition and therefore pro-fessionally, not be overpaid and not need the position for either status or for money. In order to be entirely independent, and perceived to be so, the NED should not possess much equity either, nor be overpaid and not be a former employee or former supplier. Strangely, companies would never really genuinely contemplate appointing a director purely from the ranks of those known personally to the company, so why do some still insist in doing so in the case of NED appointments? Why restrict it to such a small pool? Why assume that a company will know enough candidates, available, relevant and having the right chemistry at any one time?

At other times, a company makes the mistake of appointing a candidate because his experience is with a company with a turnover a few million pounds above their current performance. It needs to be much greater to add an extra dimension or to take into account special factors such as if the company is small but large for its sector.

The best NEDs are always curious, seeking ways of improving board processes, ensuring that the building blocks are in place and avoiding behaving like an executive director. They should understand the routes of authority in the company and check if adequate supervision is in place. The NED should choose the company as much as vice versa, and if the NED is not a current executive director, or chairman, he might become too involved. He will see a job that needs to be done, have both the time and the inclination, and before long will be behaving like a temporary executive, part-time director or consultant – everything but as an NED. Despite knowing less than his executive colleagues, which should be the case (if he knows more or second-guesses, then he has possibly been on the board too long), the best NED will be able to say "No" in a constructive way. When an item comes to the board, it is probable that the CEO and his executive colleagues will want to see the policy adopted. They will articulate well and speak with conviction. And yet if he is good the NED will, despite knowing less, be able to say "No" in such situations and his contribution will be regarded as a positive one. The NED might be requesting only a pause, seeking a time of further reflection.

As CEOs tend to be rather sensitive colleagues, not shrinking violets and needing to be constantly cherished, the NED will have to step carefully if he is not to be marginalized or ridiculed. It is a good start to know how to ask a question or offer a solution. Never say, "Why don't you do that?" but rather, "Have you thought of …?" Then be prepared to let the CEO take the credit for the idea, and be its apparent author.

At other times, the NED will need to manage tension on the board. If badly handled, tension is either absent, uncontrolled or not harnessed. It can be an invaluable ingredient, not an ugly intruder. It sharpens debate, reveals how colleagues really think and it poses, even sometimes answers, questions which otherwise the customer might do but in a destructive way!

(The NED position can be very time-consuming as well – beyond what is envisaged by the contract or even by previous experience. The number of days per se is only the roughest calculation of the true demand. For example, if a board meeting falls mid-week and the NED holds no executive roles, then the rest of that week is ruled out for holidays, curtailing one of the flexible freedoms which a portfolio is meant to offer. This is not a frivolous point when the director does not need to take on the non-executive directorship in the first place.)

Just as important, the NED will ensure that the main board does not act as if it is an executive committee. So often boards do not behave as boards and too much detail is considered, thus preventing the board from having priorities or seeing the wood for the trees. The NED is best qualified to maintain that executive balance.

Alas, all this, and more, could be of little worth if the NED does not gain the initial foothold of being respected, even liked, by colleagues. And as the boards get younger and because corporate governance is an issue of the 1990s onwards – and thus also "young" – it is illogical or odd or potentially damaging if the NED is too old compared with the average board age. If the NEDs tend to be older – because of the candidate profile, or because the candidate has been too busy hitherto as an executive director, regarding that as the priority position – it is no wonder this potential, incongruous situation can arise.

But all is not lost. The goalposts are moving and younger directors are being appointed as NEDs, encouraged officially by their own boards. To be an NED is being increasingly regarded, by both the company from whence the candidate comes and by the candidates themselves, as being an excellent – probably the best – form of personal development. It supplements formal training as a manager with practical experience as a director. It is the real thing; no contrived widget games, played in country hotel surroundings, one-off and not followed up. The NED who is also an executive director elsewhere will be on an interface constantly; as it were in metamorphosis between two roles on the different boards. At times he goes to teach but comes away learning.

The best boards go one step further, gaining even more from this shuffling of the corporate pack. They attempt to plan it in such a way that each executive director has an NED position on boards of companies representing different sectors. Hence there is an interplay with and a feeding back to the executive's board via their non-executive appointments – different layers of input.

WHAT IS IN IT FOR THE NEDs?

But why become an NED in the first place? After all, the legal downside is considerable and if one is not going for either the status or the money, why jeopardise a successful career? And the gap between executive and non-executive pay is widening at a time when the responsibilities of the NED are increasing – the committees of the board, remuneration, audit and nominations – and the downsize is being highlighted. This gap is widening despite NED remuneration increasing in real terms because of the escalating value of directors' share options and the realisation, in respect of the NED, that to overpay the latter is to curtail his freedom. It is important not to overpay the NED, even on a pro rata basis, otherwise the NED will find it difficult to be independent – he is, after all, only human and becomes rather dependent upon the director's fee.

NEDs should be mindful that they cannot, in law, hide behind the collective responsibility of the board nor will they have, in most cases, adequate indemnity cover, if it exists at all. There are wise and experienced directors who will sleep tonight believing erroneously that they have adequate insurance cover. In most cases they will not. The ceiling of cover will be easily breached, one insurance company might not want to sue another and in the final analysis, no insurance policy will cover for loss of reputation! However, to help them sleep again, NEDs in practice will not be held responsible for many actions of the board.

As corporate governance becomes more sophisticated, so the demands on the NED increase via his responsibilities on the committees of the board – the audit, remuneration and nominations committees. Ideally, when they meet, they should do so on the same day as the main board, in order to save time without diminishing their effectiveness. Perhaps the most important of the three is the audit committee and on the whole these are effectively conducted. A nifty ploy with the auditors, as they attempt to spread their risk and become more opaque when signing off the accounts, is for the NED to look the auditors in the eye and ask, "Is that the full picture?" and whether the auditors have been aggressive enough.

Nominations committees are also effective, *when* taken seriously. (The trouble here can be that the shortlist is submitted by headhunters, and the chairman of the nominations committee "sits" on the CVs for a few days, sometimes weeks. He then rejects some of them and shows the truncated list to the committee. His colleagues then complain that the list is too brief, took too long and the best by then might not be available or interested. There is a need for the committee chairman – and sometimes the committee overall – to take the NED selection process more seriously.)

Alas for the remuneration committee – the Alice in Wonderland of business life. It is an upside-down, topsy-turvy experience where corporate nonsenses are concocted, executed and barely defended by too many weak or inexperienced or badly briefed NEDs. They seem to become rather loopy – leaving their brains outside the meeting. On the positive side, a well-constituted, focussed remuneration committee can and should be a means of bringing on the best in the organisation; it becomes a management tool. Too often companies simply do not understand the purpose of their remuneration committees.

In a big company, the NED often knows only what he is told, which is what the executive directors choose to tell him. In fairness to the company, too many NEDs still spend insufficient time understanding the company. Again, when was the last time an NED visited a subsidiary to see how it operates, met those below board level to see how they think, creating good PR in the process and acting as a conduit between the board and those below it?

The benefits of being an NED are still considerable. Apart from learning by teaching, the NED will quickly realise that the other person's grass is no greener, that no business problem is unique and that he knows more than he realised even in areas outside his functional remit. Consequently it is morale-boosting and it allows the NED to stand back and see issues clearly (and even gives him the chance, strangely, to attempt the same process with the firm where he is an executive director).

WHAT CAN GO WRONG

If an NED fails, or is only a relative success, the reasons are usually because either one or other – the candidate or the firm – does not understand their respective roles. The firm will want the NED for his network of contacts and the candidate will believe he has an up-to-date one, which is effective. He would be wrong and the firm unwise to even seek such an advantage via the appointment. Networking does not work in practice; people will walk through the door because the NED has opened it, but it will not lead to anything. Rather it will raise expectations merely to have them dashed; it will cash in goodwill and waste time. There may be occasions when an NED, legitimately and practically, offers a contact as a possible solution, arguing that his source has faced a similar problem to theirs previously and so there may be a short-cut solution. Alas, networks also date very quickly, far more speedily than the average NED realises.

Others are appointed in order to rectify a technical imbalance on the board. That is mistake number two. If the board lacks a particular skill it should engage headhunters – not categorise or marginalise the NED.

Nor should an NED be appointed because he is part of the proverbial "great and good". Admittedly, fewer companies are selecting on this basis, but many are doing it almost unconsciously, either by not keeping abreast of the latest talent or by believing that those who have succeeded in the past will be equally effective the second time around and with their company – a brave and rather foolish assumption.

If the candidate is retired, or so the argument of the uninitiated goes, he will have more time to devote as an NED. Certainly there is nothing more frustrating than having a talented individual who, due to his executive responsibilities, is not often available – a problem made even worse by the fact that most companies have their board meetings clustered around the same few days at the end of the month. Such inflexibility and crowding can be insuperable, especially in the initial stage when the candidate has been approached and the board cycle for the current year has been decided.

In fairness to those who do not hold a current executive position, they can argue, and there is a degree of logic in it, that if they are on the board of, say, a Japanese or a US company, they could not have accepted these positions if they were executive directors else-where. True, but then they should not have accepted them if they were executives in the first place, and the arguments against appointing professional portfolio NEDs remain the same.

Furthermore, CEOs by definition might be too busy and chairman potentially so, thus limiting the pool of NEDs yet further. However, this does not make the retired candidate any more attractive. Once retired he quickly loses touch with the latest trends, whatever he might think. There may be evergreen, transferable skills applicable to all companies in all sectors at all times, but the subtle interpretation of those trends in the context of a contemporary board discussion can put the retired NED at a disadvantage.

The counter-argument is that he will learn on the job, might have a portfolio of appointments or even, despite the time commitment, be a chairman elsewhere and hence have an executive element in one of the appointments. True but again not the full picture, and the missing pieces are the crucial ones. Granted, the retired NED will possibly outperform all his colleagues in the first two or three board meetings, but the next few will see him repeating the same points. He has nothing to add, to supplement, to compare with, so he rapidly becomes a corporate bore. Indeed, if retired, even if he is still quite young – and this is, as noted elsewhere, an increasingly likely prospect – the NED might be tired or not sufficiently motivated or the factors which previously combined to facilitate his success may not come round again. He was lucky and is no longer so.

Another potential cause of failure to appoint successfully is to believe that an NED with a portfolio of NED positions is up-to-date, is much in demand and so is likely to be a good addition. In practice, the other positions might prevent him attending the other board meetings and will invariably not constitute a total or meaningful experience for the NED. It will be rather superficial and his efforts scattered, resembling a rather fussy CV. (It can be equally unwise, though, for the candidate to become too selective, wait for a supposedly better offer and merely be left on the corporate shelf.)

There are even companies that appoint one of their advisers to the board as an NED. It is daft to appoint such a person; why change a winning horse and complicate relationships? If the adviser is good at advising, keep him in that role. Unfortunately, some companies cannot resist the temptation to meddle and confuse roles and the results are usually disappointing. If a company really does want an NED with a particular skill, even if they accept that he can and should contribute across the wider range of issues, then at least appoint a different person from the same sector and have the combined input of the two.

The worst mistake is to appoint from a pool where there is no choice; only one candidate, recommended either by the company's advisers or by a current member of the board. No choice is an unnecessary risk and awkward for the candidate, if appointed, who will then feel beholden to the person who recommended him. It is far wiser in the long term to leave a position vacant rather than fill it with second-best. Wait for the right person. In the meantime, the current talent needs to be managed.

Some companies panic in their selection, know their own warts, think they are less attractive as a result and then offer too much money or too generous a remuneration package – one that some candidates feel unable to walk away from and so compromise their independence. Let both sides choose each other and the rest will normally slot crisply and seamlessly into place.

Maybe the contract of employment is too generous or counter-productive – if, that is, such a contract is offered in the first place. Surprisingly, many companies still fail in this fundamental and basic way. The contract needs, among many things, to offer employment which is on an annual renewable basis, not three years and then a further three. Otherwise the independence or flexibility of the appointment is further curtailed. One of the benefits of an NED appointment is that it can reflect the changing needs of a company more easily than changing an executive director (and, incidentally, offer continuity if the executive directors come and go). So why forfeit those considerable benefits? By the way, if the NED is below standard his contract can still be terminated with only one month's notice because NEDs are not technically employees, something most companies and NEDs do not realise.

Another mistake can be appointing the NED straight to the chairmanship. This usually means that the succession planning has not worked out correctly and the new chairman will have a lot of sorting out to do – changing the strategy rather quickly, publicly and under pressure – never a good base to conduct reasoned debate. Better for the candidate to be appointed as chairman designate, either officially or preferably unofficially, letting him emerge as the heir apparent. If this is not to be, little is really lost. He will still probably make an excellent NED in that firm.

Sometimes the wrong appointment is made because the NED has joined a sector in which the wool can be pulled over his eyes, usually unintentionally of course (though for those few companies that object vehemently to good corporate governance, sometimes intentionally). The usual sectors with such complications are defence and ones with a significant public procurement element to them.

As in other aspects of the corporate scene, where success and failure can be only a thin line apart, the NED might still fail. It is difficult to know if a board is working effectively when one is an executive director; how much harder it is when an NED!

A CHECKLIST

The NED can increase his worth and personal satisfaction from the appointment if he follows a few specific and rather simple principles. He should do due diligence, assessing viability, on the company and the board as individuals – even then it might not produce all the answers. Most accept the opinion of obvious sources – the firm's accountants, lawyers, a few City contacts – when further probing is required. On occasion, an otherwise suitable candidate is rejected because he asks too many searching and thorough questions at interview. The fear then is that he will interpret his NED role as an executive one. This is unfair. All the candidate is doing is conducting some due diligence. After all, the best appointments are made when both sides select each other and the selection is made between equals. A thorough probe and preparation is essential and should be regarded as a compliment or, at least, a sign of sincerity.

He should ask the existing NEDs how they were appointed, how long ago and how much briefing they are given. In fact, does the company really believe in corporate governance and is it willing to brief the NEDs to make them effective? Then the matter of chemistry is crucial; it is not merely what the NED says but how he says it and whether the board will accept contributions from him. Furthermore, both sides need to understand their respective roles and the NED will need to know when to comment and how to comment. The noisy ones, who believe they are judged partly on how much they say – hopefully good quality contributions but likely as not, not relevant to debate – and empty vessels can become very tiresome.

Over a 12-month period, there are possibly 100 issues on the board agenda; only a few are crucial and the NED needs to ascertain which they are and which ones he can help most with.

From the due diligence will come an assumption or belief that the chairman is either an effective one or merely rather ceremonial. The best chairmen will encourage debate, and that includes NED contributions, and the very best chairmen appreciate that they are leaders of the non-executive team on the board when the going gets tough – the senior team, evolving from the ranks of the board. A good chairman encourages discussion, not mere presentation.

To succeed, an NED might have an independent additional source of data, a source allowed by legislation and encouraged by corporate governance reports. Whether he should be permitted to speak to the City, as a right – having notified his board if, in extreme circumstances, he deems it necessary – is a more moot point. On the whole, if the actual original point was a fair and constructive one then the answer is "Yes" – because something pressing needs to be aired. (There are some voices advocating that NEDs should have a formalised and regular contact with principal shareholders. Perhaps such an idea will be of limited worth and could disrupt the board's workings and even divide the board.)

Certainly, it would be advisable for an NED to know how the Stock Exchange marketplace works. Shares overreact – both up and down – but relative performance, against their own share price and that of others in the same sector, is a healthy indicator of the shape and condition of a company. (More NEDs, more often, should interpret their role as being a champion of the shareholders.)

HOW TO BECOME ELIGIBLE

If the position is actually rather exciting and is made for the right reasons, as defined above, how does a director become an NED? First, he should not leave the exercise until the day before retiring as an executive director, believing that the world is waiting for his call and will understand why the candidate has precluded himself previously.

However busy, the executive director should seek his first NED position at least by his early forties. By then if he has the attributes he will be ready. Then the executive and non-executive careers can run in parallel with the latter coming to the fore as the director reaches retirement. If the candidate is too busy now and asks the other company, or the headhunter, to come back in five years' time, the pursuer should pursue with added vigour. The candidate will be fully abreast of current corporate developments and might, once introduced properly to the NED scene, relish the prospect.

But then there are some who, however successful, might still fail to be attractive enough. Most companies require those with executive main board, plc experience. There is no substitute; it is where the buck stops, where the ultimate decisions are made. Others fail because they have been with one company too long and so lack the wider corporate perspective, however much their company has changed in the meantime. Others – such as consultants, the military, politicians and academics – all find it very difficult to secure the NED position that they desire, most believe they deserve and some truly warrant.

Although an appropriately appointed NED is a form of cheap consultancy, the two roles are very different in practice, both psychologically and legally. Members of the military simply lack conventional or comparable skills, however much Whitehall has changed or they can argue that, in practice, the armed services are really like a commercial organisation. (It is rather unjust in their case because they have at least been consistently successful.) Politicians, even those who have held office in business-related departments of state, have not become businessmen. They are politicians.

Academics also lack the necessary experience, and the litmus test is that very few have actually become NEDs, regardless of their academic reflections and original research. There is an undeniable gulf between academia and business. Participants in the former try to make issues complicated, because their world seeks and probes for the full picture or to view from new perspectives; in the case of business, however, a director needs to understand in order to make decisions, simplifying in order to understand.

There is room, though, for the unconventional appointment if the majority of the board is conventional – there is a need to act unconventionally and think outside the corporate box. There is room too for the hybrid candidate who can add a new dimension. This person could be younger and may have no main board experience, but knows how to probe, represents a different generation and is a pleasant colleague to have on board.

Women have had a rotten time breaking through the glass ceiling. As mentioned in Chapter 6, some have been lucky but are undeserving of their success; others are unlucky and we all need their day to come, and speedily.

SPECIAL FACTORS, TAILORED NEEDS

If the NED is to join a smaller company or a family firm, additional points to bear in mind include having to devote more time than usual, possibly helping the founder exit from the firm. A prospective NED in this situation needs to check for himself how much real influence and power the NEDs actually have (does the power reside in the family and are non-family people merely appendages?), and how to resolve the question of equity – for the family, not for himself, as there is little prospect of acquiring that. Also, he will possibly find his roles more blurred than in a larger plc. Finally, NEDs on such boards do sometimes find it hard to control the executive directors in general and the family in particular, while some of their decisions might seem somewhat wacky to a third party. It can still prove to be one of the most rewarding places in the NED constellation; it just requires extra deliberation prior to taking up the appointment and a certain understanding of, and sympathy for, the family.

If the NED is appointed at the time of a float, a few extra factors must also be considered. There is a special need, and the onus here is on both the candidate and the company's financial services partner, to ensure that the board believes in the role and that there are no skeletons in the cupboard. There is a reluctance among some boards at such a point to believe that the NED can be other than another unnecessary or unproven overhead, additional to what they are used to, imposed by their advisers and making the company the conventional organisation the executive directors escaped from in the first place. And financial advisers might put pressure on the NED, if appointed at this stage and as an appointee of the City, to have a hidden agenda and not be a standard appointment. Financial advisers will almost certainly want to exit early as well.

If the NED waits until after the float, possibly to be reassured that there are no skeletons to emerge, it could be too late. The institutional pressure for the appointment might be off.

If the company has a big corporate governance department – and some of the larger companies are gradually establishing them – they need to justify their existence and to do so they are prone to ask their advisers plenty of questions; many of which are of only limited practical value.

Finally, whatever the original apprehension, despite inauspicious rumours and the official view that the legal downside can be so great as to make it unwise to ever seek or accept a non-executive directorship, few have ended up in jail (fewer than perhaps should have done) and most, most of the time, regard the experience as fun and fulfilling.

3
THE CITY

The relationship between the City and main boards is often one based on confusion, animosity and undue deference of the latter to the former. The deference is reasonably easy to understand; it is based largely on ignorance of the workings of the Square Mile. It is one of the peculiarities of UK corporate life to allow the brightest directors with very few exceptions to avoid all contact with the City prior to joining the main board. Once in their elevated and crucial position, they might be asked to brief those who present to the analysts or, worse still, talk directly to them.

Arrayed against this ill-prepared corporate soul are the skilled ranks of able, articulate, knowledgeable and possibly rather arrogant individuals. The mystique of the Square Mile exists almost solely because of the inability of companies to prepare their high-fliers. There is nothing inherently daunting about financial service firms, apart from their fees – fees allowed, accepted and meekly paid by the client, who accedes to the argument that there is an international rate for the best; companies have to pay their employees that rate to retain them, hence the client eventually picking up the bill, or so the argument goes.

THE PSYCHOLOGY OF THE SQUARE MILE

Let us peel away the mystique, layer by layer, and create a more meaningful – though no less expensive – relationship with the City. First and foremost, there is a psychology to success with the City. A company needs to understand what the financiers are actually requesting or expecting. Obvious? Then why do so many companies either give too much information or too little too late, or present it in such a way as to create mistrust between the two? In fact, some companies do not even know what they have to offer to themselves, their customers or the City, for many do not know how to manage their own intellectual property. Hence they do not know their full worth.

There is a need to strike a balance with the City for sometimes it is obligatory or appropriate to reveal only a small amount of knowledge of a company's intentions because of commercial sensitivities. However, there is a great deal of cumbersome, unnecessary and neurotic behaviour in respect of what is confidential and what is not. (Some firms even send invitations or Christmas cards marked strictly confidential! It is usually the professional firms, but not exclusively so.)

The City wants companies to try to achieve results which are, at least, slightly better than expected or forecast. On no account should a firm attempt to hype its forecasts or be unduly pessimistic. Again a balance, a tiptoeing, through the corporate maze is essential. It is not always easy; the unexpected can genuinely happen and the City dislikes the unexpected – there may be a defaulting client, a key director could leave, or a host of other reasons – there is no degree of care or well-honed behaviour that can mitigate against all the vagaries of business life. The firm might be given an assurance by the finance director of a client firm that a potential debt has only a low risk rating, but the debt can still occur and subsequently it will possibly have always been a more dubious potential debt than the firm was led to believe. Yet at the time there was probably little the other firm could have reasonably done.

However, there is still undue hype on the part of companies about their performance, masquerading as a perceptive prediction. People, and therefore companies, have a propensity to look on the bright side. There is a fine distinction between wanting to put a gloss on the figures – aided and abetted by professional PR firms – and pure hype. The dot.com boom is a perfect recent example of hype. Companies that grow fast and believe they will maintain absurdly ambitious rates of growth are another example. If they marked time just for a moment, they would quickly realise that no company can realistically maintain such momentum. If it did it would be unique and would overtake all the competition; eventually, no doubt, equalling the total market share available in its sector. That supposedly seductive scenario is quite absurd in practice. Such companies are, in essence, refusing to accept that a trend is a trend and a cycle cannot be outwitted. Then there are those who revert to type not because of abnormal growth, but because they are doing rather badly.

It is hardly even argumentative to say that trading statements are biased by a ratio of at least 25:1; most forecasts are worse in practice than predicted. A warning sign for the City and shareholders is when a company says it is preparing to make a trading statement! That usually means that the figures are poorer than the original hype. The share price falls as a consequence.

What often makes the City disgruntled is when a firm regards a downside as merely cyclical when it is potentially a major problem and should be regarded as such by the board. Or when the board does not share a profit warning with their bankers. There is a need for transparent trust. Or again, any revised numbers given to the bankers need to be realistic and fair. In practice, revised forecasts are often over-optimistic and are given at least three months too late! Usually, there is a four- to six-week critical period between the realisation of a problem of this nature and doing something positive and relevant about it. The NEDs have an especially important role to play in such circumstances, but it is one they often ignore or fluff. They should ask the basic questions, persistently and fearlessly. Is the dip a temporary one, or more prolonged? Banks need to know for the sake of relationships. The NED needs to check and reassure himself that the company forecasts are not over-optimistic.

Obviously, banks want to resolve such potential pitfalls, avoiding possible nightmares. A trouble for their client is a trouble for them. Surprisingly, clients under pressure become petulant, defending their own mishaps by blaming the banks. It is necessary to remember that banks are commercial entities and their first priority is to their shareholders, and that might, on occasion, not necessarily be to the longer-term benefit of the client.

But are banks fair-weather friends? Certainly banks want to protect their own financial exposure. Sometimes they will put pressure on clients to hand surplus cash back to shareholders and the client thereby becomes exposed. All rather silly and taking no account of the obvious fact that a financial situation can change – and very quickly. (Not only can a cash mountain evaporate because of bank – or City – pressure, but directors are also just as able to eat through it, quickly and with relish.) Directors can foolishly succumb and act on a whim or be sidelined.

It can be exceedingly hard to maintain a working relationship with bankers for any reasonable length of time. Personalities on both sides come and go, pressures such as those just referred to affect each partner at different times in the business cycle and to greater or lesser intensities. Even if the client attempts to talk to their bankers in confidence about perhaps, a profit warning, it usually leaks out.

A corporate equivalent of the litigious nature of everyday life is the increasing need to employ professional advisers, especially when in trouble. Then the dispute is a contest between equals – albeit achieved at a heavy price. At least though with an accountancy firm on side, all those concerned, including the banks, will have a greater degree of confidence in the numbers presented. In the final analysis, clients should remember that no company is too large, or too well-established to avoid being toppled by its bankers.

Clients complain that the institutions are happy to see them when things are going wrong, but not when they are going well. Usually the City does not deny this but argues that in an ideal world, of course, they would keep in regular and meaningful contact, regardless of the circumstances, but that they do not have the time, especially in the growing global marketplace.

Yet advisers should find excuses to be in touch with their clients. They should find reasons to knock on their client's door in order to evaluate an issue or even to discuss a national one – such as the consequences of the single currency, even if not adopted in the UK

(75 per cent of the FTSE 100 companies have had no visit or com-munication with their advisers on the likely consequences to them of this momentous decision). To visit only major clients, and then infrequently or only in times of crisis, is a bad policy and poor management – time will pass, a problem will fester, an opportunity will be lost.

If it's a small or medium-sized enterprise (SME), a firm will have the problem of not being known in the City, which in turn will not undertake a great deal of voluntary tracking of its performance. The SME forgets that the analyst probably has at least 60 other clients in his portfolio. Unless the client is very special, big or lucky, the analyst will probably think of the SME only once or twice every two months or so.

The SME has a further almost impossible uphill task if it expects the City to understand or choose to understand all the innuendos if they are planning a rights issue (incidentally, a float and a rights issue have a parallel – both need to deliver their promises). The City will be even less enthusiastic, their concentration span more restricted and they will just yawn if, on top of all else, the SME has a small market capitalisation – which, by nature and definition, most do.

However accurate were the previous forecasts or predictions by the SME, the City will largely discount them as history. The City will buy only on the reality of its performance, not on the promise of future successes. Larger firms operate at a distinct advantage, therefore, over the SMEs in this crucial respect. No wonder many smaller firms fail to push themselves through the various stages of corporate growth to reach the bigger league.

A good trick for the SME, or for the firm unknown and apparently unloved in the Square Mile, is for a director to enhance his reputation by using his own money to buy back his shares. This is interpreted by the financiers as a good portent and they might just act more warmly and co-operate more willingly with the director concerned and with his company. Understandably, and surely rightly, it is not regarded as the same if the director merely accepted shares under an option scheme.

Largely forgotten by SMEs is the equally important aspect of how to deal with the Stock Exchange – and with investors generally. The SME needs to ask itself what the City is looking for from them, and what are they allowed to do under Stock Exchange regulations. It is pointless and fruitless composing a presentation pack to institutional shareholders if the SME, through ignorance, addresses the wrong issues.

THE SHARE PRICE

Companies often complain that the City does not understand them and that this is best reflected in the way the share price moves. Indeed, there are many chairmen – and CEOs – who are acutely frustrated and more than a little annoyed that the share price often does not reflect the true performance of the company. If the company has not explained its performance and aspirations, then it is most to blame, but often the company could do no more and yet still the City harshly and routinely punishes the share price. In a way, the share price is as much to do with managing expectations as it is about true performance or maintaining sustainable value for shareholders.

An added problem for the analyst occurs when the company has a high profile. Unrealistic expectations can be attached to it; unfounded self-belief in a sustainable growth record or in having a sure touch all play a part in confusing the analyst or, more likely, making his audience disbelieve him. Awkwardly, there are occasions when the board knows what actually should be done but cannot take a hit to achieve it – the shareholders expect quick, constantly improved returns. This is one of the conundrums of corporate life.

Currently, there is not the quality of analytical research in the UK compared with the USA. Hence, if not a major player, the company will be adversely affected by poor coverage by the analysts and this, in turn, will subdue the share price. If the chairman and/or the CEO and/or the finance director are also inexperienced when dealing with the City, there are present all the ingredients of massive misunderstanding, acrimony and confusion. There is a mutual responsibility for all relevant participants to help ensure that the share price reflects reality.

The majority of shares quoted are traded sparingly. Most shares are not very liquid, unlike in the USA and, therefore, it does not need many shares to be traded to move the share price.

Sentiment influences share price movements, and if only a couple of analysts follow a particular stock, and they meet in a wine bar, and one says to the other that he is going to sell, the other will not wish to be out of line. Economics has little to do with it. Sentiment does. There is a formula; the more analysts who follow a share and the greater the liquidity, the less clubby the situation, and possibly the more realistic the share price.

There is one way of playing the City game and gaining a temporary, yet effective PR advantage and, in so doing, to help to control the sentiment attached to the share price. If the company is expecting bad results, it might be advisable, and possible, to announce them on a Friday, or when a major company is scheduled to announce its results! Furthermore, it is a skill worth appreciating and then refining to know how to influence the City quietly behind the scenes. Too few directors appreciate the value and power of gossip and intelligence; in corporate finance they can be the deciding factors. Play the game, avoid becoming too much part of it, and by so doing steal a march on the competition.

Raising money in the City is a much easier exercise if the company concerned has a good story to tell – and that usually means raising money for the benefit of the shareholders. (A board should not do anything unless it benefits the shareholders!) Too often directors fail to understand this casual link between the City, the company's directors and the eventual outcome of a money-raising exercise. Pure logic, hard work – perceived necessities as viewed by the board — are not necessarily enough; the directors also need to appreciate the psychology, the sentiment, the agenda and therefore the priorities of those who have the money to lend but who, otherwise, might not have the desire to part with it.

In the case of shareholders, from one viewpoint the firm need not be unduly concerned. The majority of shareholders – over 60 per cent – do not bother to participate in the firm in any way whatsoever. They are mute investors. Even this is a mixed blessing, however. It can lead to unexpected dangers. First, the minority will still exert undue influence, disproportionate to their numerical strength as expressed in their total equity holding. Second, companies need to communicate more effectively with their principal shareholders. They probably have only about 20 of them, so it is hardly an onerous task. Only then can a board buy time. It also means telling the truth about the current situation.

It is odd, perhaps, in the light of the pocket-sized number of main shareholders, that companies spend so much money and time on advertising or PR, attempting to influence a wider audience. Why bother when the firm will know who the small audience is and where it can be found? In short, the best companies have learnt one crucial lesson in respect of share price movements which their less successful brethren have not. They have a culture of loving their main shareholders, finding ways of keeping them content, on side, keen or at least patient towards the board's aspirations and performance.

It is very easy to feel sorry for the small shareholder. Together they might constitute the majority but their voice is fragmented and often belittled or ignored. Conversely, the big single investors, usually the pension funds, hold sway. And yet to them the stake might account for only one in a large portfolio. The individual shareholder will have greater personal risk and exposure and less influence. It is really up to the NEDs to represent their private investors. Alas, few do, and even fewer realise that it should be one of their responsibilities to do so! (Incidentally, the status and performance of the pension trustee, despite official nudges, remains manifestly unsatisfactory. They allow others to take their cuts – the advisers, the administrators, etc. and meanwhile, the trustees themselves remain a relatively lowly part of the multi-billion pound industry, deciding the financial future of untold millions.)

Befriending the analyst, while crucial to the wider perception held of the company, is not a one-off exercise. Analysts come and go. At the peak of their tenure, analysts can gain great job satisfaction and hold sway. But they have a shelf-life, perhaps at most of ten years. After that, they recognise the business cycles and it becomes rather tedious, unstimulating, even boring.

Furthermore, analysts have another characteristic, on this occasion particularly frustrating for the client and poor form generally.

Analyst reviews never mention corporate governance or board composition or processes. This omission is dire. If more than a decade after the first corporate governance report, and all the accompanying debate, it is difficult to know what actions or events will precipitate a more sensible and constructive response from the analysts in this area.

Neither does the City appreciate too rigid a script, whether companies are raising money or merely presenting to them. They prefer a natural approach with the emphasis on insights, on how the figures, the year and the strategy are likely to pan out. Again, the City will be looking at the right amount of figures and data, but also for good results and no shocks.

WHEN THE STAKES ARE HIGH

If the company is floating, a whole tranche of new rules or attitudes needs to be considered. Normally on both sides of the float, the City requires more information than usual. The demand will then recede as the company establishes itself as a more conventional plc. Furthermore, the immediate post-float time can be an especially crucial period for the client. The City still has big expectations and has equity to sell, offloading shares as and when it chooses. Another factor at this stage – and for how long will depend upon the maturity and sophistication of the directors – is for the firm to appreciate the difference between public and private capital. So often the regime in charge at the pre-float stage is *in situ* afterwards and for too long, failing to understand that whereas previously the monies they were responsible for were probably their own or that of the family, now the money belongs to a more catholic-based shareholder portfolio.

There is also a lot of glamour attached to a float, and this can cloud judgements. The NEDs especially will need to be seasoned and be able to tell the executives, especially the CEO, how the board should be developed, updated and strengthened, in order to meet the challenge of being a plc. Their financial advisers should add their voice to how the board needs to develop. Most do not bother; they are by then onto their next deal. The float should be regarded as a milestone in the corporate history, not a joy-ride to riches. It is little short of a corporate rebirth.

The secret of a float is not necessarily to do the mechanics of the float well – there are plenty of technically qualified people around to do that – but rather to convince potential investors of its competitive and investment advantages. As the directors become increasingly enmeshed in the float – or MBO/MBI – they will learn incredibly quickly on the job, exhausted by the dipping of a toe into this largely unknown and possibly very hostile, time-consuming exercise. To them it may be the first time they have carried out the exercise. To the City it is one time out of many. For the client it means learning but also conducting normal business with the same vigour and determination which made the firm sufficiently attractive to float or buy out in the first place. To take their eyes off the corporate everyday activities is to court disaster. The value, price and overall attractiveness of the potential float evaporates. Once this has been realised and fully appreciated it is likely to be far too late to stop the process. The directors will have gone too far down the route with nothing to show for their efforts should they terminate the exercise prematurely.

A float can help the directors understand their business better. There are directors who believe they know all about their companies when they do not. Often they are neither conversant with nor abreast of the figures; they have not grasped sufficient detail. In routine times they will skate over such issues and seem, in the short term, to have got away with it. Their arrogance or complacency will return to haunt the company. A float, meanwhile, is an admirable way of educating the directors in financial realities – as long as the float is justified in the first place!

In short, going through a float makes a man of a director, eliminating the bucketful of naivety that they had originally. If most realised how taxing and demanding the entire process would be, most would never commence this important journey. Thankfully, due to their naivety, they do not, and corporate UK benefits accordingly. After all, a float/MBO/MBI is all part of the corporate evolutionary process and many floats work in practice, with a ripple of benefits that reaches many a distant shore.

And, by the way, if the director is attempting an MBI, it is a distinct advantage to be thick-skinned and to choose a finance house which knows the sector especially well. It even helps if the director can convince the City that he is going to be involved in the new corporate entity, long term and possibly even full time.

Often a potential MBI has problems, which at the time look either insuperable or so great as to make the deal too risky to contemplate. And yet this may be an unnecessary jaundiced view, allowed to gain the upper hand because of ignorance and panic on the part of the directors. Many of these "insuperable" problems can be curtailed and managed, even marginalised if they are nailed down quickly and if the MBI is executed at the right price. Unfortunately for the directors, if the company is being well run, it will demand a particularly high price. There are bargains around but money does not grow on trees. Any company wishing to become a client of the City, and especially when contemplating acquiring a company, should remember that however competent is their presentation, however proficient the due diligence and however motivated the management, there are few well-run companies today which can be purchased at a competitive price. Gone are the days of the bargain.

It is critical that the company does not feel committed to purchasing a particular company regardless of price. The general rule is – pay good money for good companies and little for bad ones. Remember that if a company is planning a hostile bid it will pay a high price only when it knows that it can make significant savings. Remember, too, that investment bankers are transaction-driven. They have little or no interest in the longer-term future of the company. What they seek, and often almost demand, is the best price, which is the highest price. Almost as simple as that. The client, in turn, should pay only a fair price and be brave enough to say "No" if that price is being exceeded. The psychology is rather like an auction – know when to say "No".

In the specific instance of an MBI, the City will need even more convincing before they will back the deal. Many of those directors in the potential client company will look good and have a sound record but will suffer from not being single-minded enough. Often those involved in MBIs are serious and determined and it is largely up to the bankers to assess their ambitions in a more prosaic and dispassionate manner. In the process, the City can appear overly cautious and lacking in appreciation of genuine entrepreneurialism. In fact, those involved in MBIs can often be people who cannot tolerate the disciplines of conventional firms and they will go to great lengths to disguise this simple reality. They will try to avoid the formal strictures and in so doing they can, in fact, be merely looking for a job or be chasing rainbows. A bit too harsh, maybe, but the assessment is not without truth. This is doubly depressing when one is reminded that the senior management team is the key to a successful MBI. And if or when the company has corporate lift-off, its problems have only just begun.

In the case of any major business transaction, there is a need to keep one's feet on the ground. As a company, the "more" realistic and exciting is a business prospect, the more clinical and detailed should be the company's assessment. Unfortunately, often the reverse is the case. Even when all is progressing well, some fundamentals must still be taken very seriously. Risk profile, for instance, should take a centre stage. It is also important to ensure that the company has the necessary financial data and knowledge of existing controls present in the other company.

Getting relevant data can be difficult, and made impossible by inadequate checklists. It is often not acquired in time due to ignorance of the need to obtain it in the first place. Furthermore, if a company is keen to expand, many of the early deals are done on a whim instead of via a properly formulated strategy so the company might not have a culture of adequate due diligence. The added discipline might hold up the hitherto rollercoaster acquisition ride but it is worth the wait. Notwithstanding the possible logic of acquisitions or mergers, a company must still have a strong organic business which it recognises, cherishes and is prepared to invest in. It cannot avoid the running of the business by making acquisitions.

Oddly, though, a company can possess all these attributes but in the denouement of the exercise of a takeover or whatever it can still often be a matter of feel or of a finger in the air!

Too many recent City clients suffer from the inherent pressures which subsequently force all but the most resilient teams asunder. The team will be keen, united and confident at the time of the float,

ring-fenced by a consensus on the strategy and looking optimistic-
ally at the distant sun-drenched horizon. It is wise, though seldom
done, for a team wishing to float or do an MBO/MBI to talk to
another that has been through the process before, as long as the
team is not necessarily put off as a result. (One of the problems
facing the City is to determine when a potential deal is a serious
prospect or merely a matter of posturing. No wonder the City, in
self-defence and in order to justify its fees, sometimes argues that
most deals do not come off and they waste a great deal of time on
futile ones. Analysts are under pressure as well!)

Many acquisitions, therefore, are of companies that are in dif-
ficulty; otherwise they would not be for sale or not at the right price.
Remember the simple trap laid for those who have failed in a much
sought after bid. Nine times out of ten the same directors combine
and become determined at the first opportunity to find another
potential victim. They become almost desperate for the next deal.

WHEN DEAL-MAKING

It is rather pointless to approach the City if the intention is to make
a series of small acquisitions. Better by far in that situation to
attempt to grow organically. The company can then control all the
levers and, in all probability, create more wealth via sound financial
and managerial controls. Alas, some directors do not like that
approach; it is not very exciting, original or sexy! It is the harder,
slower grind to efficiency. But it is the right approach in that
instance, nonetheless. Often it is safe and successful to move
organically and cautiously, undertaking an initiative on a small
scale at first and then perhaps a number of other small-scale ones,
building up from a well-prepared seedbed.

Indeed, many acquisitions end in disappointment and failure. They do not deliver and those responsible in the firm are protected by the remuneration committee and by their lax terms and conditions. The City is not unduly bothered either; they are paid either way. Corporate UK is the loser, with the loss, in all probability, of a potentially successful piece in the business edifice, a precious block picked up and discarded.

In fairness, some companies with a strong balance sheet and good management can afford to take the occasional punt as long as the financial commitment is not too great, but remember that when making changes of some magnitude the company will need to protect its existing business in the process of these massive and often sudden upheavals. It is easy to lose what you have got and upset those around you.

A company will also be judged by the Square Mile on its professionalism and acumen in respect of making disposals. So often the spotlight is on the acquisition but the tidying-up of a corporate portfolio is just as important.

From one viewpoint, it is almost possible to feel for the City, or at least to understand from where they come, however bruised or disillusioned a corporate player might have become! In banking, in deal-making generally, the City can lose money even quicker than it can make it, and its reputation in the process. It can take years, if the time is offered in the first place, to claw and clamber back up the corporate pole. And the constant accusation of short-termism thrown at the City is not entirely fair. On the whole, short-termism is the fault of the investor; it is they who demand the returns. The City is the medium, the institutional method of achieving the investors' short-term goals. This situation is made worse if the client will not listen to his financial adviser. Only two things can then happen: either – and this is the more probable outcome – the client will listen in the end, or there is little point in the adviser retaining that role, and he stops having that firm as his client.

(Interestingly, many venture capitalists rely on their tame, conservative, aging lists for the appointing of NEDs to their investments and in so doing miss a crucial opportunity to ensure that their considerable investment bears fruit. They are not even aware of what they are missing, and yet the talent out in the corporate scene is encyclopaedic. Furthermore, a company of any size can just as easily lose a bid because it does not know anybody in the City as for any other more sophisticated reason.)

In many cases the price of a transaction is largely a question of whether the firm is buying or selling. Price can also have a determining effect on the subsequent attitude of directors when managing and absorbing their successful acquisition. If a company has to offer a high price, especially in a hostile bid situation, it will expect to make considerable cost savings later. (In the case of an MBO, in particular, it can be a question – but this is becoming rarer – of an opportunity arising largely because the corporate headquarters of the company of which it is currently a part does not know its true value!) Sometimes a company predator will be arrogant and consequently lose, even to a competitor offering a smaller price. The former will probably have failed spectacularly to keep close to the seller during the period of due diligence. Meanwhile, the company offering the lower price might have been carefully explaining what they would do if successful. This is more prevalent in the case of private companies. The larger plcs find it increasingly difficult nowadays to avoid selling to the highest bidder.

The company will be at a disadvantage vis-à-vis the City if it is a conglomerate or is structured in such a way as to have loose links between its operations. It can be successful and ambitious, but the City will mark it down, largely because the Square Mile chooses not to understand such structures nor the sentiments which, in the eyes of the directors at least, warrant it. Pressure comes from financial services to become more conventional when this is not necessarily best for individual companies. Conglomerates are also viewed by the City with mixed feelings precisely because they can be split up. The best defence for a conglomerate wishing to remain as one is to take the company private.

Sometimes a conglomerate should purchase additional businesses in order to attach them to existing ones with the intention either of making that part more attractive to sell or so that economies of purchasing power can be achieved for core parts of the group.

Whether aiming to raise money, or wishing to float, or merely intending to keep the City abreast of developments or of hopes or even of corporate fears, a company needs to establish a relationship with the City of such quality that, in the eventuality of trade turning sour, it will have a more sympathetic audience. It is futile to expect co-operation and leniency when the horse has bolted.

CITY FIRMS ARE POORLY RUN

With the City, it is not a matter of winning the argument via sheer logic; a company has to win its heart as well. The company's fate can be in its hands, whatever the logic. Unfortunately for the client, the character, structure and nature of the City firm is often so very different from their own. What is happening, therefore, is that the two "sides" – the client and the City – are less similar to each other than they appear or believe themselves to be.

First, they are not actually comparing like with like and the same language can mean different things to the other; hence one of the reasons for the souring of relationships. Second, City firms, on the whole, are poorly run. They are a collection of very able or less able people who, regardless of their true abilities, believe they are all very accomplished and conventional with terms and conditions to match. Many are little empires, run in ways that have changed remarkably little underneath an exterior that has made them appear a different species altogether. Their real structures and attitudes mark them out as less than qualified to succeed in the current global marketplace. Those closely involved – whether City firm or client – do not actually realise this.

The majority of the City's bright and most impressive fee earners do not supervise more than half a dozen staff. They are ill-qualified to assess the managerial talents and depth found in or absent from a client's cupboard. And yet they make investment decisions and charge their fees as if they have conducted the fullest possible exercise in due diligence. They will also claim and believe that, in practice, they are very interested in the quality of management and not just in finance and capital. In short, the technical side of a finance house may be very strong – it is the management and leadership which can be, and often is, weak.

Be that as it may, it is a pity that they lack practical managerial experience. In the case of venture capitalists, there is at least an advantage to the client emanating directly from this imbalance between technical and managerial skills; because most of the former do not know how to run businesses, they will not want to be the majority shareholder! That does not mean that the venture capitalists are not ambitious. They will want to invest in an enterprise which itself has ambition and a growth story.

The much vaunted internationalism of the Square Mile has largely meant, in practice, the Americanisation of it – a process which went on concurrent with the revolution in information technology! Consequently, the City has changed beyond recognition, but not in ways that either the City or others necessarily appreciate and not to the degree that each assumes! No wonder doing business in this area can be a question of the blind leading the blind. We should not get too carried away by some of the more recent trends. The City has a long and proud history of welcome to foreign ownership and influence – Germans, Swiss, French and others have long found a lucrative foothold in the Square Mile. Wisely, the City has encouraged the best, regardless of their national origins, and largely, in recent times at least, allowing US culture to win.

THE NEW YORK STOCK EXCHANGE

Because UK companies are tempted to become involved in the USA, and feel that they understand the US psyche, especially with the Americanisation of the London financial markets, we need to spend a few moments assessing the reality of the US financial services.

There are many subtle and more obvious differences between the two financial markets either side of the Atlantic – and the UK director needs to appreciate these, be ever cognisant of the differences – and these are in addition to the plethora of non-financial differences between any two countries, referred to in Chapter 4.

In the British financial scene, London dominates and most UK firms have their corporate head offices either in London or nearby.

There is a compactness. In the USA, political power resides in one place, financial power in another and corporate head offices can be 3000 miles away from either. It would be interesting to contemplate how many Fortune 500 companies have their board meetings within 100 miles of New York. As a percentage, certainly far fewer than do the UK with London. Most US directors would neither have grown up near nor be especially familiar with New York.

What a contrast with the juxtaposition experienced by their UK counterparts, and yet from one viewpoint, the Square Mile is less cosy. In New York, and to a much greater degree, the relationships are between the company boards and the investment houses, a relationship which extends back over generations. Oddly, therefore, despite the Americanisation of the Square Mile which destroys many meaningful relationships, in New York those relationships, in one form or another, survive.

Moreover, the reduced status of the London Stock Exchange has further widened the differentials in how to trade within the two respective financial markets. In the UK, the Stock Exchange does not even approve listings any more, unlike in New York.

And there is a further difference and complication. Boards in the USA are more representative, more democratic, with more women, ethnic minorities, etc. It is a greater manifestation of the harnessing of available talent.

There has been a reaction in the UK, at least at the margins, against the deal-driven culture of the USA; hence the establishing of financial boutiques that will offer a different perspective, and perhaps a longer-term one. They are not necessarily paid to make a deal – unlike the US-orientated approach – and are valued the more as a result. Their prevalence and influence should not be exaggerated; they are not major players in the Square Mile but nevertheless indicate a strong desire by some to seek a more balanced traditional and non-US approach or contribution. Indeed, their role has been given a boost by the current debate on conflicts of interest and the role of advisers, whether accountancy firms or the big City players.

THE CITY'S OWN AGENDA

Whatever attitude directors have towards the City, they need to remember that those working in the City are mostly only advisers. They are not at the heart of the management of their clients' organisations. Moreover, on the whole, the City operates to an agenda which is both different from, and would not be the first choice of, the company. The City wants dividends and will put pressure on management to pay them, whether they have been earned or not. It will also encourage a client with money or the facility to make lucrative deals to do so, even if the deal might not be in the longer-term interests of the client. And yet, peculiarly, the City nearly always regards a price paid by a company for another as too expensive!

If that is not challenging enough, the City will also have certain boxes it wants ticked before the deal is considered, beyond the usual diligence covering the basic figures. For instance, if two companies merge or one takes over another, the City will look for evidence of a balanced team, with little or no acrimony, other than healthy relevant debate. In short, the City likes to see harmony. As an important aside, mature industries are partly in another category all together. They are not, by definition, growth companies and, in the eyes of the City, there is insufficient scope for investment. What the City does, in these circumstances, is to put pressure on the company to make acquisitions or to diversify, all in the name of performance. Alas, from the company's point of view the City's attitude here is all wrong.

Additionally, the City needs to have faith long term in an existing team. It helps to achieve such a relationship if the client's short-term performance is satisfactory. (A note of caution here. There is a difference between the proverbial short-termism of the City and the City's desire, even insistence, on assessing a management team for its long-term capabilities on its short-term performance.)

A satisfactory or ideal relationship between client and City will depend largely on the chemistry between the leading players, just as is the case when composing the management team, especially the NEDs, in the first place. Ultimately, it is crucial for the firm to have advisers it can trust and then to know how to use them effectively. That comes with experience and a short cut to acquiring that familiarity is to appoint an NED with just such experience, albeit remembering that the best NED appointments are those who are generalists first and foremost. Astute directors choose the individual rather than his firm, finding a person they can work with effectively.

PERSONAL REPUTATIONS

Unfortunately, after the satisfactory concluding of a deal, the City can be rather inflexible in its assessment of individual directors, even bigoted and unrealistically cruel. Some City firms will damn or enhance a reputation, offer an imbalanced reference and cause a great deal of mischief, without an ounce of reasoned logic. Some-times, and this is at least rational, the City will give an especially good reference to the director on the other side of a deal.

Occasionally, the attitude of the City towards an individual director and, to a lesser extent a company, can be difficult to fathom. Some ride their luck, are the golden boys on the corporate block, can do no wrong, are given more time or a second chance and are even offered fulsome references for the next job. Alas, for others the curtain falls. The boardroom and City doors slam or click shut, never to open for them again. There is plenty of luck, as well as of course at other times logic, in respect of which City institutions have a good word for a particular director and company. (It is a very small world; if a director manages to acquire a bad reputation – and he need not have done anything illegal, merely gained a reputation as a peccadillo or a charlatan – he will more than likely end up in the corporate wilderness.)

The potential client needs to realise that, however important they are in their own eyes, however enthusiastic and infectious is their message, the City will make less money out of a deal involving them if the deal is relatively small than if executing a larger one – the time involved in both cases being about the same. (Interestingly, the City tends to play one more game with their clients. Whatever sort of relationship has been established between the client and the City, the latter, on specific occasions, will introduce a specialist, a technician to carry out a particular job. He will appear from nowhere and soon will disappear again.)

If the firm is small or medium-sized, and has negotiated a win fee arrangement, then the directors should be cautious; they might have concluded a Pyrrhic victory. The client should question their agenda. Who are the City advisers really working for? In addition, a potential client will not find the City very co-operative or understanding if it wishes to raise money ultimately in order to resolve a problem. Rightly, the City will believe that the potential client is asking it to throw good money after bad.

Once a deal has been concluded, the finance houses show remarkably little further interest in any aspect of corporate governance. This is despite repeated requests from corporate governance reports, anecdotal cases strewn across the business pages and the inability of many, possibly most, remuneration committees to put the interests of the shareholders before those of the directors or ever to consider the interests of the small shareholder. With few exceptions the City could not care one iota. The deal has been made, they will be paid, and a deal-maker is only as good as the last deal. To complicate the issue further, these self-same deal-makers are often only a group of individuals thrown together, working for themselves and for their bonuses. They are rarely a team. In the case of merchant banks, and to a lesser extent with venture capitalists, the process is often a ritual of the deal process! For the venture capitalist, the pressures are, if anything, greater still. The individual has only about three years to prove himself if he is lucky. In fairness to both the City and to the NEDs it is wise for all concerned to apply the corporate governance code with a light touch.

It would be wrong to assume that the interests of the City and those of their client are inherently different and that it is a question of playing a game, hoping to beat or fool the other. While there is sometimes an element of that, if a deal ends in failure or a company subsequently goes into liquidation, there is usually a good reason – wrong product, wrong place, wrong timing. If the problem was "merely" bad management, then that is a different matter, but the City is still not the one to be blamed. At least if the cause of failure *is* for a good reason then it is a waste of time trying to save or resurrect the company. If not, there is every reason for considering doing so. Either way, the City will not be the fundamental reason for the debacle.

It is worth remembering also, and from both the City's and client's perspective, that it is not necessarily a bad thing to have some debt in a company. It keeps directors under pressure, on their toes. It is the understanding of that debt, the harnessing of the energy it can generate, which are the keys here.

Sometimes involvement with the City is both unplanned and unwelcome. A company may become successful but in so doing it becomes tasty and a bid might be just around the corner. Naturally, this could, in turn, mean riches for the founders, the principal shareholders. But the approach could be very unwelcome; both the price or the timing, or both, might not fit the agreed strategy. In that case, a new skill will be required by the defending company, one necessitated by success needed to mitigate the adverse consequences of good performance. The board will need a director or two who have both the time (if an NED) or the skill (if an NED and/or executive director) to fight or at least to obtain the best deal.

The relationship between the City and their clients is one of the most fascinating imaginable. It is also one which both sides have made harder for a constructive result to be achieved in a positive and friendly manner. Blame is divided between the two.

Despite the criticism of the City by those wishing to do business there or who feel they have been misunderstood in the Square Mile, or who feel simply unloved and unappreciated by financial service companies – and despite this truer picture of the financial services sector – the City remains successful on an international level. Indeed, in the abstract, the United Kingdom can be relatively proud of its financial services.

4
TRADING INTERNATIONALLY AND WITHIN THE EU

Corporate life is littered with abortive efforts either to establish an overseas presence or to replicate overseas what has been achieved in the UK without fully appreciating the many potential pitfalls. The odds against succeeding overseas – or within the EU – are possibly greater than those for succeeding. Furthermore, there has been a scramble for companies to acquire other companies and many of those are located overseas or within the EU. Again, it is a hazardous strategy and one littered with mistakes and disappointment. However, their subsequent prospects need not be so slim.

A GLOBAL VILLAGE FULL OF POTHOLES

Above all, it is both arrogant and flippant to assume, as many companies do, that there are more similarities than differences between countries. Often the differences, whether subtle or not, can be considerable. One need look no further than the USA. From the business perspective, it is not one country, nor is it even merely 50 separate states but rather an amalgam of four distinct regions – the Eastern Seaboard, Texas/Deep South, the Mid West and the Western Seaboard. To assume that they are the same is a recipe for disaster on a par with the corresponding commercial arrogance, tempered by ignorance, in which the USA, in turn, often regards the rest of the world, and in particular the EU. EU countries are not an artificial, recent establishment with no history or separate identities. Indeed, there are examples even closer to home. The UK regions differ from each other and have more in common with each other than they do with London!

But going international is different for different industries. For instance, quarrying is the same everywhere, whereas consumer markets have different dynamics in each country due to their differing cultures.

If the CEO has a dream, is determined to expand overseas, and his board have either encouraged him to do so or cannot dissuade him from pursuing that target, then certain fundamentals need to be borne in mind. There are stepping-stones to be traversed, with caution, and after much deliberation, if a company is to survive, let alone benefit from an overseas or EU venture.

Should the company merely trade with or should it have a presence in the country? More frequently than many corporate strategies would suggest, the answer usually is to trade but not to establish an office or manufacturing base. Even merely trading within the EU or overseas requires a disciplined approach and thorough homework. The exercise will, almost invariably, be more expensive and complicated than originally perceived. It can also prove unexpectedly expensive to establish a business in the rest of the EU if the company does not own the whole subsidiary. While the rewards may be there the potential pitfalls and downsides invariably are.

For instance, limited liability is different between countries; get that wrong and the CEO will not remain in office. Or again, the company will need to contemplate being ensconced for the longer term; otherwise there is no point in embarking on the original corporate odyssey. One routine mistake is to blunder into another country, believing erroneously that they can get healthier margins than is achievable by companies in the UK.

There is the need, in addition, to understand the national psyche. From the business viewpoint if a businessman thinks the French are the same as the Germans, or that either is more than superficially similar to the British, then the learning curve will be long and steep. On paper, as viewed from a pristine corporate headquarters in either Bracknell or Reading, the benefits of having a presence in a particular country are blindingly obvious. Apparently, the market is there, the skills are available locally and there seems to be a reasonable degree of political stability. But there are hidden costs or disguised traps waiting for the unsuspecting. It may be cheaper to employ staff overseas, but what happens if the self-same staff need to be made redundant? How complicated are the local employment laws? What degree of protection do employees have? What knock-on effects will the decision have on other countries in which the company operates? (On the whole, the rest of the EU has more "advanced" employment protection legislation compared with the UK. But by "advanced" it means more inflexible, comprehensive and making the conducting of business on the Continent more expensive and less attractive than in the UK – although the UK is becoming less attractive and more similar to the Continent by the day.)

And that is just the beginning. The world might be getting smaller, a global village emerging, but the world can become suddenly very large and hostile. Perhaps it would be better, after all, to acquire the plot next door in Bracknell at a higher relative cost, both in land and labour. At least the management will know all the rules, and it could be simpler or much cheaper in the longer run and they can look out of their window and see what is going on.

This so-called global village – in which apparently we all live and which we are told will manifestly become smaller, more homogeneous and easier to comprehend – is not actually either succinct or tidy. It is a corporate labyrinth and if all was according to the textbook we would not get overseas expansion so wrong, so often. There are common links between foreign countries but there are also significant local differences, which need to be recognised and respected.

The company will need a strong base, a real presence, otherwise it is too risky. It is not a board game for two to six players to be enjoyed and then to be put back into the games drawer. It can constitute make or break, for the board, their reputation, the City, the shareholders and the employees. A lot can and often will be at stake and, with the multiplier effect, the knock-on commercial ripple, the numbers involved for good or ill can constitute a mind-boggling gamble.

If it all goes wrong you might assume that you can sack your management and transfer production to the Third World; however, not only will the employment laws make it expensive to do the former but your competitors can always do the latter. There is often no real competitive advantage in such a transaction. Usually, it is essential to let indigenous nationals run the company locally, at least at the most senior levels. (Some successful businessmen argue, energetically and convincingly, that if a company is playing away from home, not only does the grass appear greener, which is an illusion, but also, if playing there, then put only your very best people in. "Pursue this argument," they say so ardently, "even if it damages the business at home in the short term." To operate overseas – and this can equally include the rest of the EU – requires maturity and effectiveness from the players to a peculiar and demanding degree.)

In the initial stage, you will need people who you know, can trust and, above all, who can understand what they are meaning, not just what they are saying. For example, in the USA, business-men tend to be more positive and optimistic than their UK counterparts. To the Americans, the glass is never half-empty, only half-full. It is important for the home team to interpret the messages without any degree of ambiguity – hence the need to engage senior, UK nationals who the US representative understands and believes at this crucial stage!

Nor is it easy to find the right employees to run the overseas activity if they are to be relocated from the UK. They need motiv-ating, having an eye kept on them and being given a re-entry route – if they can be persuaded in the first place to move at what could be a crucial time in their lives. Their children may be preparing for national exams and the dog could be too old to put into quarantine. Colleagues will not necessarily realise what the employee has experienced, how he has changed, that is if they can remember him in the first place. Not everybody in an age of the non-corporate career relishes an overseas posting, being with foreign nationals. It is on a par with the problem of selecting and locating those previously destined to serve the Empire. The fact that many did it successfully – whether escaping the law, their families or whatever – should give the corporate world some comfort, even if companies, on the whole, are recruiting a different set of skills! By the way, every company should be attentive when dealing with their CEO who is based overseas. If he is the wrong person, the company needs to act very quickly, even more speedily than in other situations.

DEGREES OF COMMITMENT

However, even before any of these worries need fill the minds of those around the board table, there is yet another preliminary step to take and a precautionary note to sound. Somebody will need to suss out the overseas situation beforehand, in order to ascertain who among his colleagues, or what skill set from outside, will be most conducive and acceptable.

If the company is having second thoughts about an overseas presence, yet still wants to enhance its business with a particular country, a possible solution is to establish a franchise arrangement. At least, it would not be your money or people! Or establish a joint venture.

What a relief that there is this in-between type of overseas presence. The company can own part of the venture, have a real presence, not via an intermediary and not as a virtual reality sort of company, which is not so satisfying to the CEO nor reads so well in the annual report. But joint ventures can be shorthand for corporate disaster. Who will take the leading role? The one with the biggest investment or equity stake? How long will the arrangement last, or when will it be scheduled for renegotiation? Which employees will be best suited to sit on the joint board?

Perhaps the joint venture might offer one or other partner new ideas. But it is always at a potentially heavy price. Most joint ventures do not remain in their original form for more than about five years at most. What happens when the original signatories leave their respective companies, and the character changes, the chemistry alters and new players are acting the script? A safe view to adopt is to say that unless there are huge opportunities, especially in the USA, do not do it. For joint ventures to be successful, however qualified or modest is the intention (and this applies equally if the joint venture is purely UK-based), there will be a need for both the culture and the strategies to be in unison when often only the strategies are. The answer? At least put in writing as much as possible and thereby avoid some of the future avoidable problems.

Yet words can be interpreted differently and joint ventures usually ignore the golden rule – they fail to include an exit clause on day one. One side will have to be prepared to become the reluctant senior partner even if that was not the original intention. Then, just conceivably, the joint venture will be the appropriate medium for your company at that time and in that part of the world.

Another potential downside of a joint venture appears if the exercise needs more money and one partner says, "No". The other company involved might – and in all probability will – attempt to go off with the technology and have the ultimate control. In the process the other partner will have been offered, almost on a plate, a practical and valuable yet cheap start-up.

A joint venture need not be finite in time; there is a difference between a business joint venture and a project joint venture – how much capital for the one rather than for the other, how liabilities have been assessed, and how realistic and perceptive are the procedures to manage them properly and profitably, and so forth.

Other necessary clauses in the agreement will be to cover cases of breach, of unilaterally breaking the agreement (let one side do it if they must, but ensure that there is a penalty for doing so). In fact, all this initial negativity has another beneficial effect beyond avoiding the avoidable; it helps the parties to the agreement to know each other better. Remember, also, that it is better to be cynical here and to assume that most of the financial data supplied in the early stages of the negotiations will be inadequate. Invest a little extra time and effort, beyond the information offered by routine due diligence, to ascertain the fuller picture. It is rather like taking out a more thorough survey before purchasing a house.

Finally, joint ventures often fail because the decision-making is harder and the activity covered by the agreement is not a core one in the eyes of either party. The lesson here is clear; treat this corporate solution with respect!.

THE USA

More specifically, there are certain fundamentals to note when trading in particular parts of the world. It is wise to begin with the USA, easily the most interesting and important in both the psyche or in the reality for the average UK firm. Americans tend to adopt ideas faster than the British do but, alas, they are also likely to discard them more readily. In the UK, we take longer to adopt and to drop. Furthermore, with the USA, there is a tendency for them to force their culture on others when trading, regardless of where the company is situated. Strangely, the Americans still have an inability to understand that the world is both a diverse and larger entity than even their own country and this despite the flexible, gifted and energetic nature of many Americans – living in that vast, eclectic, melting-pot of nationalities. There are US companies still that plan their overseas approach with a presentation starting first with the obligatory quote from Mark Twain and then explaining that the company wants a chunk of the EU to become, with a magic wand, a new 200-square-mile European region, as if they were recreating Wyoming, Utah and Montana out of France, Britain and Italy! The lines thus drawn will be arbitrary and will cut across national boundaries and cultures. "Bad luck," say the corporate Americans, "we want it that way."

For the UK company, unless it intends to have a reasonably large presence, there is no point in attempting to establish a lucrative foothold in the USA. It is the big country, full of opportunities – and full of potential pitfalls.

Then there is the challenge thrown up by attitudes and expectations. In the UK the majority of people spend most of their commercial lives in only one or two companies – surprisingly perhaps, considering the ups and downs and major changes in UK corporate life, especially over the last 20 years. In the USA, on the other hand, people change companies more frequently. The result is that the British may begrudge moving, and their US counterparts will probably relish it. In addition, it is important to appreciate how Americans behave, even dress, and also to understand their humour and their one-liners. It is said that the common language divides us and it is never more true than in the commercial sphere. The result is that there are few UK-registered companies operating successfully in the USA – especially ones run by UK nationals. Safer by far for the British in the USA to be in control of the next tier down.

Different employee expectations between the two countries manifest themselves in additional ways; incentives versus basic pay, contracts of employment, benefits, discrimination, role of trade unions, etc., all adding to the US corporate labyrinth.

Britons who excel "across the pond" ultimately depend on how at home they feel in the US corporate culture, and with its local variations. The director needs to embrace the culture of the other country and on a personal basis.

The naivety based on the isolationism of the USA has cost their finance houses dear. In recent years in particular they have lost many millions of dollars, and often the losses could have been avoided. But the USA will persist in viewing the rest of the world as a little extra beyond the self-sufficient, all-pervading structure of their own continent.

Despite their confusing approach, which borders on the arrogant when trading overseas, much of what the USA does and how they do it is to be admired. They do not waste natural talent in ways that the UK persists in doing. For instance, many US businesswomen reach higher levels of management, having started their careers as PAs.

Being the largest trading entity, the USA has two peculiar characteristics for the UK. We feel drawn like a magnet, lured by its corporate size, diversity and potential rich pickings, and UK companies often feel that they are missing a commercial opportunity if they do not have a presence there. Such influences are potentially extremely perilous; companies must never be bamboozled.

The similarities between the two countries are less than the differences and the former are, unfortunately, easier to note and even feel, than are the latter. Before even looking at a map of the USA, UK firms will need to be specific, and be able to quantify their objectives for entering the US market. And then a whole raft of questions will need to be posed and answered. What is the perceived competitive advantage, the intended timeframe, the criteria against which the UK firm should judge its sortie into that marketplace?

Each of these questions – and of course, there are many more, leads to questions of levels of commitment of staff, capital, time, etc. And there are, conceivably, 50 different sets of criteria to consider because there are 50 separate states, each with their rules on competition, consumer protection, public procurement and even acceptable techniques of lobbying. Moreover, there are factors of scale, distribution, diversity, regional and national business cycles, and the well-known but wretched litigious nature of US life, which affects employment, the environment and consumers.

The US cultural melting-pot has a direct beneficial spin-off into their corporate activities. The USA is no longer, of course, an Anglo-Saxon nation. It has a large, important Spanish element and less-publicised German and Italian components. For the Spaniards, Germans and Italians, trading in the USA is becoming easier and may, in the not-too-distant future, become as easy – or as difficult – as it has been for the British – or, looked at from another angle, thereby making it even harder for the British. Our commercial advantage, despite English being the commercial language of the world, is less outright than it was and will be even less so in the years ahead. (And by "language" is meant also its usage. The Americans expect and respond to a degree of directness, even exaggeration, which the UK does not practise. To be quiet, diplomatic, circumspect and subtle will elicit a nil or vacuous response from a US counterpart. They will not understand what is being said or expected of them, if they realise that they are being addressed in the first place!)

The USA is also a more practising Christian society than contemporary secular Britain, with a large representation of all other religions. It is therefore both a multiracial and multireligious society.

However, not all the historical advantageous of being a UK-based firm have been eroded in the process. There is still, despite fashionable talk to the contrary, an innate bias in many areas of the USA for those with a UK background.

The open, flexible USA does not have a monopoly on entre-preneurialism – if anything the balance is coming this way across the Atlantic. Britain can be proud of its entrepreneurs, both in their number and quantity. But before the champagne corks pop, the Americans are better, much better, at offering adequate financial backing for them. US entrepreneurs are more ambitious than their UK (and EU) counterparts. The American entrepreneur will ask for over four times as much funding as will his UK counterpart and then the latter will compound the problems, by taking a different attitude towards risk and failure. In fact, in the USA, the heroes are business people – the magazines are full of how to be a millionaire or an entrepreneur, to them often the same thing. There are more business heroes, more business legends than the Wild West ever fabricated, and most of them are pleasanter folk.

In fact, the USA is even clearer and cleverer in respect of their entrepreneurs than that. Their venture capitalists know how to establish a worthwhile relationship with their universities. More-over, in the USA, there is an assumption that the latest star in the corporate firmament will be the new kid on the block. The sun will shine over his halo – until the next one emerges. How very different in the UK, where often the opposite is the case.

Interestingly, the average age of a UK entrepreneur is about 45 – not the very young as portrayed in the media. They are not the very young – and over 90 per cent are men! (There is a frustrating philosophy in the UK, unlike in the USA, of not wanting to select the best talent and back them to the hilt. In practice, it is important to operate a successful anti-elitist policy, whether for the universities or in any other naturally competitive situation. It is not logical to wish all universities were top when they are not and cannot be. The hypocrisy of some in the UK, especially of the self-made, is beyond the pale. Managers of Premier Division football clubs, anti-elitist to a man, usually self-made and rather chippy, speak of being anti-elitist yet practise elitism most with their own football teams/businesses. They constitute an embryonic version of a national psyche.)

The best universities in the USA welcome a visit from a venture capitalist. They understand the potential relationship and positive advantages to both sides. In the UK, disputes arise over intellectual property rights and probably even over car parking places as well.

The budding UK businessman also needs to be alert to other factors. The US markets tend to be more price aggressive than our own, and service is a criterion that comes high on their judgemental tables (although perhaps the difference in practice is somewhat exaggerated).

Finally, there is a difference between the two countries in respect of where power lies within a company. Some UK CEOs look enviously at their US counterparts where, unlike in the UK, the CEO is king and his equivalent NEDs are little more than rubber-stamps – that is until things go wrong. Then the rubber-stamps will bounce back and sack him! There is some evidence that the UK is going partly the same way. The NED remains strong and is getting stronger but, at the same time, the CEO is also being given a greater role – until matters go wrong and then the CEO is also dismissed.

AND THE REST

Generally, the EU can be split between the North and the Mediterranean countries, but the generalisation is fraught with exceptions and consequential dangers. Northern EU countries may be nearer to us psychologically and geographically but there are small, yet significant and potentially fatal differences. For example, because the climate is slightly colder in Scandinavia than in the UK, in the rag trade, fashions and expectations are subtly different. Even the pattern of trading can vary. In Germany, for instance, a "northern" EU country, Saturday afternoon trading is only a recent phenomenon.

The Germans, on the other hand, can also be rather poor at running their overseas subsidiaries but for different reasons. Again they too do not take full account of local factors when trading internationally, but in their case, for a special reason. The Germans now "suffer" from not having the successful and broad colonial past that Britain, and France and Holland to lesser extents, acquired. It is important to emphasise the inherent advantage of a former empire in contemporary commercial terms. Even relatively small modern Austria has an in-built advantage when trading with the growing economies of the former Eastern bloc simply because of the former Austrian-Habsburg empire. The British are the most fortunate, however – they are able to trade comprehensively and truly internationally – not with Europe (their colonial history is peculiarly unhelpful in that respect) but with two-thirds of the rest of the world.

Incidentally, the Germans tend to prefer to be managed by other Germans or by the French rather than by the British. Why? Possibly because they do not like our desire to downsize and constantly seek change. This is another example of a problem raised before, in another situation, as it affects another country when trading internationally, but is based on a different reason, and with a different outcome. It is easier to play chess against a grandmaster than see a successful way through the chequer board that reflects the various countries of the so-called global village.

The Germans also have a different timescale and career path from other nationals (although there is evidence of a convergence), in respect of employment. They spend longer at university than their UK counterparts (despite the gap year and its supposed attractiveness and long-term benefits), and retire earlier. In Britain by the age of 30 the employee will have had, on average, seven years' practical experience, and then retires later. So Germans will operate with a different labour force both by age and expectation. Not a huge difference but a subtle one.

To give only one paragraph to Italy is not being dismissive; the fact is few foreign nationals have much experience of management positions there despite its relative size, because large chunks of the Italian economy are still largely family- and privately owned.

The French are a problem! There are few UK directors who have had constructive, effective, non-frustrating trading arrangements with French companies. Even here, there are ways of reducing the obstacles. Whereas in the USA, for example, there is often only a short debate before a decision is taken, in France it is more a question of exhaustive debate, discussion and further discussion. (Both situations, in their different ways, create problems for UK businessmen.) Overlaying all, and especially the case in respect of the linguistically sensitive French, the role of English as the commercial language of the world is a red rag to the French corporate bull.

When doing business in France, the secret is to have good local partners. Almost above everything else, this is a magic key to a more successful, happy and grown-up relationship. (In France, by the way, it can prove costly and legally cumbersome to exit. The cost of exiting can be more than setting up there in the first place!)

Psychology plays a larger part in trading with France than it does in most other countries. The perceptions of French people of themselves in private and in business life are almost seamlessly linked. The French are clear about a number of things – they "know" most about eating, women and fashion and it is almost pointless for another country to do business with them in these areas, and to assume that the French will believe that the trader has anything to offer. It is probably worst in the area of fashion. Alas, it is also difficult to assume what the French say is what they mean – at least to an Anglo-Saxon mind. A contract means almost nothing to them; they will sign it and then ignore it. The deal has to make commercial sense and stand on its own, to have any merit or legitimacy in their eyes. Alternatively, one can always attempt to bribe the local mayor; if successful, fine; however, unsuccessful ones could find themselves in exceedingly deep trouble.

That is the situation if the foreign company has bothered or been able to reach the signing stage. Before that, it might have dawned on the potential trading partner that French red tape adds up to 50 per cent to the price of doing business there, and this on top of a difficult French attitude, a different market and the cost of opening (or closing later).

With Japan, lesson number one is to appreciate and accommodate the fact that the Japanese are culturally very different from most in the West (and from many elsewhere as well), and that their manner of conducting business, however successful, is equally different. To ignore the subtle innuendos is a sin and an expensive one. Furthermore, great patience is required. It may take years before a consensus is reached but once achieved it sticks, unlike in the UK where apparent consensus is reached rather quickly but it can buckle or break readily under pressure. Equally, Japanese body language should be understood. The Japanese will give an answer even when they do not know, in order not to lose face or for reasons of politeness. In addition, because of the lowly status of women in Japanese commercial life, it is usually diplomatic, however unpalatable, to negotiate with the Japanese and regard it as a male-only exercise. (In Japan, there is an overriding need to behave correctly. The way a person conducts his business there requires a lot of briefing and preparation. There are no short cuts). This may be the 21st century but the Japanese still adopted a different approach.

In the Far East generally, but Japan in particular, most deals are done largely by word of mouth; little is written down. Detailed agreements are rare. There are many ill-prepared UK business people who will stroll through the Japanese corporate business jungle with their eyes firmly shut. Generally, those from the West cannot understand those from the East and vice versa!

And do not forget that the Japanese want market share whereas the West tends to want profit. Nor forget that to trade in the Far East generally – and with Japan equally – involves complicated distribution routes and warrants the need to operate via a trading company. Remember, also, if trading with the Japanese, not to expect quick returns – long-term partnerships are the order of the day. (The Japanese are changing rapidly, becoming less Japanese in outlook. The Japanese tourist "with his camera" equals a traveller, which means a degree of awareness of how the rest of the world thinks and operates. The younger Japanese, in particular, are dissatisfied with the business regime which lasted until the late 1990s and served them well – but no more. They realise, all too urgently and keenly, that the venture capitalists need to play a bigger part in the evolving of a truly international, open, flexible, Japanese economy, one which is more likely to sustain the inevitable buffeting of world trade. For UK directors well versed in corporate governance and in the role of the venture capitalist, the future should be being drawn up in their favour.)

Moreover, with the Japanese, you must never show weakness, nor become impatient. (To add a trip to Hong Kong while in the region, there are other stepping-stones to negotiate, a further trap for the unsuspecting. Hong Kong operates at many levels of business culture. If you employ one person, their relatives might expect jobs as well!) On the academic front, countries in the Far East prefer to have contacts with individual professors rather than with their universities. This is mainly because, and perhaps a little surprisingly, in Japan university organisations are not that impressive.

There was a hint above that not all Westerners are so very different from the Japanese. The one exception, surprisingly, are the French. Arguably these two nations are rather similar. Their education and decision-making processes are not so very different from each other in practice. The main ambitions in both corporate cultures is to please the boss – unlike that appertaining in the "Anglo-Saxon" culture. Further, both the French and Japanese appear on the surface to have a collective, consensus approach, but in reality are rather military and dictatorial. In both corporate cultures, one person is in charge.

In addition to there being general characteristics attached to one country and worth noting by all other countries wishing to trade with it, there are also additional factors specific to country X when it trades with country Y. For instance, the Japanese complain that the Americans neither listen to them nor take the time to form relationships with them. And, incidentally, most countries believe often erroneously that what is "right" for a business in their own country is regarded as equally "right" elsewhere.

BEHAVING INTERNATIONALLY

More generally, it is difficult to successfully transfer and replicate UK niche operations to other countries. Or again, it is worth remembering that international companies, in an era of growing globalisation, can be larger than many national economies. Who do they answer to and how powerful are they in practice? Can technology make national borders almost meaningless? As a rule, national governments have a disproportionate influence and so punch above their weight despite their relative smallness, compared with the international players.

Just as each country is different, despite having many characteristics in common, there is a whole raft of different factors to bear in mind between different sectors. Take engineering: few engineering companies are international or are leaders in their chosen markets.

Often international companies are domestic companies with overseas operations run on the parent's domestic lines. If the nationals from the parent take all the senior posts, it is a multinational. If indigenous people are in charge locally in different countries, it can be regarded to all intents and purposes as an international company. If the company has a large array of overseas outlets, in different countries, it is important to remember that they should be managed according to the local culture. For example, if your firm has a presence in New York and Dhaka, the two places have virtually nothing in common from the commercial standpoint.

Incidentally, it is quite impossible to manage a group that trades internationally if the operation and product or service are different in each country. The group's future is in being broken up, for nobody at the centre will understand the concept. The fragmented entity will then operate successfully as individual local entities. A multi-country presence is fine, and even commendable if the product is the same or mutually compatible.

One point, which is hardly ever highlighted, is that it is still difficult to ascertain the true performance of various subsidiaries overseas: there is no agreed, comprehensive and universally adopted auditing procedure across the world despite the larger international accountancy firms merging mainly in order to be global. The audit remains fragmented and rather meaningless from the company's angle and from that of the shareholders. In fact, it is even more complex. Non-commercial factors play a major, often determining, part. When dealing with governments, the company needs to understand what terms are necessary in order to secure an agreement. And yet – oh dear – in Italy there is a model which works and almost disproves major tenants of the government/ business relationship. Business people there, including entre- preneurs, survive despite the government structure! There is a rich, varied and enviable array of world-class and global brands which are Italian (and often private, second- or third-generation family affairs, thereby throwing many otherwise sound business assump- tions out of the window).

In most parts of the world, for the British to do business on a large scale necessitates permission from the foreign government and even some involvement from the UK Foreign Office. The

Foreign Office, much criticised by UK businessmen, realises this even if many companies still do not. Indeed, most UK companies are politically naive. They do not know when, or how, to lobby; whether it should be at local government, Whitehall, Brussels or via their trade association. There are factors which do not respect the variable idiosyncrasies of different countries. For example, a national government should never forget how internationally mobile companies can be today. Governments need to treat them respectfully in areas such as regulation, or they could lose out to a more willing foreign competitor.

Some countries are probably less than fair in respect of international competition and therefore in allowing others to set up a business presence within their borders. Countries such as Switzerland – civilised, European, safe – can achieve unfair competitive advantage by putting extra legal obstacles in the way of conducting business by foreign companies. (As with the USA, so with Switzerland – there are a number of countries or very distinct regions within the national borders. There are three Switzerlands!)

Do you still want to trade overseas? Incredibly, despite all these and other challenges, Britain owns more of the world than the world owns of the UK, and the UK percentage is growing annually.

As international trade develops, there will be concurrent developments reflecting the need to accommodate the global scene. The solutions themselves can lead to further challenges. For instance, the globalisation of international boards has produced some peculiar and haphazard solutions. Some boards will appoint one foreign national as a non-executive director, but there are at least three distinct corporate governance models and the three are not remaining static either. The UK model of the unitary board, which was developed via the corporate governance reports of the

1990s from Cadbury to Turnbull, is exciting interest elsewhere. But that does not mean an uncritical adoption of all the insights now encaptured in those reports nor some of the sentiments behind them. Directors and companies are not comparing apples with apples. In the USA, all but the CEO are NEDs ("external directors"); in continental Europe with its supervisory boards and a nudge towards UK corporate governance, the picture is hazy and somewhat hybrid.

Germany is in the vanguard of continental European corporate change, due to legislative amendments since 2000 and as a result of the psychological jolt created by recent unprecedented foreign takeovers. However, Germany might be amending its corporate governance rules with alacrity, and setting a pace among its continental colleagues, but it is still developing a different model from the Anglo-Saxon one and it remains in a poorly developed state overall. AGMs, for example, are noticeable for their lack of private shareholders and for the large numbers who attend. A Siemens AGM can expect 7000 to attend, albeit largely employees who enjoy the day out, and will not generate much critical debate. Consequently, Germany approaches its international and even European trading with a different set of role models and from a different historical basis. Appoint an NED from Germany, for example, and your problems might just be starting. He may not understand our language, our body language, our corporate governance procedures, or the Square Mile. In fact, not only will the foreign national possibly not understand the City; he might well not understand any other foreign nationals on the same board! (Many UK companies that operate on an EU or international dimension are too British. But to put foreign nationals on their boards in order to rectify this is not an easy or logical solution.)

The boards evolving at present to meet the globalisation challenge face other distractions as well. They may be large – especially if the organisation is the child of a merger, acquisition or takeover. Also, there will be cultural differences.

Possible ways of mitigating these problems are fraught with further difficulties. Reducing the number of board meetings, or meeting at different locations around the world, are not answers. Boards are meeting less frequently, whether a global player or not – it is merely sound business practice. Meeting at different locations is rather cosmetic, resolves only a minority of problems and is merely following existing best practice. Modern technology looks more promising – but it is not yet sophisticated enough and there is the inherent question of confidentiality; plus, of course, the inability of technology to convey the feel, reactions and subtle innuendos that can only be felt if physically present. Integrating two companies from two cultures blurs board decisions. Investors, whether institutional or private, want a strong representative board. The global board which achieves that is the exception.

Furthermore, the truly international company can be quoted on 18 different stock exchanges around the world. How many active investors will hope to keep track of their investments and accept the extra challenge – further compounded, by the variable auditing standards?

At least the Japanese, with their very different corporate culture, have made the board structure a little easier to understand for the UK businessman or investor, but by default. The Japanese have been very slow to globalise their boards. But do not jump on the next plane to Tokyo. Most Japanese boards do very little; the real decisions are taken elsewhere, by committees!

On a slightly light-hearted note but on a matter which, if misunderstood, can have big consequences is the subject of giving, when visiting overseas companies. There is an art to giving – to judge the level appropriately. Not too much, not too little, whatever is regarded as relevant for that particular country. Perhaps a major UK department store could produce a guide. It would save embarrassment and lost opportunities while, hopefully, preventing the company and the director breaking any laws.

In fact, business people trade overseas or within the EU at their peril if they ignore the different organisational structures found in various countries. Power lies in odd places.

5

SMALL AND FAMILY FIRMS

Increasingly, the small or smaller firm, whether listed or private, is becoming ever more fascinating as a concept, a vehicle for the entrepreneur or for those who prefer to concentrate on perform-ance rather than merely profit and shareholder value.

What is "small"? One of the most profitable definitions is: "You are small if you think you are." More specifically, a small company is unlikely to have a current annual turnover exceeding £250 million. The other characteristics, both obvious and less so, plus their relative importance, will be considered below.

Undermined by governments, via creeping bureaucracy, despite public utterances to the contrary, the butt of comedians if the firm is in the hands of the third generation or more, small and family firms remain responsible for more job creation than their larger brethren and are increasingly fashionable for the ambitious.

What is so endearing about these firms? What characteristics do they display? Why have they survived the age of the large corporations? What makes them, to a peculiar degree, the chosen base for the unconventional, the educational drop-out, the proverbial simpleton and the corporate role model of the young? And why is it that too frequently, for the good of either the bigger firm or the smaller one, they do not make much effort to understand each other? Moreover, why is it that the bigger companies, despite everything, have an appetite to devour the smaller ones and yet in so doing, often get indigestion or skulk away, unsatisfied?

A FASHIONABLE CONCEPT

Over the final two decades of the 20th century, larger firms became less attractive as a career path, hierarchies became flatter and employees did not view a career in one company as a corporate path for life. However, the larger firm remained, to the more discerning or conventionally educated, an excellent initial preparation for subsequent business life, offering the inescapable disciplines needed in order to run their own or somebody else's enterprise. Merely to demand meaningful management accounts, on a monthly basis, with sufficient detail, is almost axiomatic, and this type of schooling is offered virtually exclusively via the larger firms.

Once with the smaller firm, but only when it is via the previous experience of working for a larger one, the director will have a platform on which to perform, and an opportunity in which to excel and in ways he could not have done previously. The smaller firm offers the business person a degree of executive freedom, an escape from the procedures of the bigger firm. It is the sensible ones who recognise that, with success and growth, certain of those additional structures will need to be introduced as a cruel necessity. Not too many, not too soon but some nevertheless. It takes a disciplined director, a strong but tactful NED to see a small growing firm through that crucial adolescent stage. (Incidentally, if the company is very small – i.e. the director is self-employed – he will have yet another advantage over others for he will have no internal or indeed infernal meetings, which will therefore free him up at least 40 per cent of his time. Quite an advantage!)

With a smaller company, there are fewer staff, relationships are closer and all have a better chance of knowing what is going on. There is an immediacy with clients and colleagues, an ability for a director to go onto the shop floor and talk to colleagues, thereby ascertaining the pressure points. A message, an order, an instruction, fear, anything can go to everyone within the hour. That is good – and valuable – feedback!

The smaller firm is more flexible and can respond to circumstances more easily. Directors attracted to the SME environment realise this and it will be one of their reasons for being with a smaller company in the first place. They can also appeal to the rather unconventional; when a company is small, a director does not necessarily need to – although, of course, he should – function in conjunction with others in the firm. Such directors do not learn to delegate!

What is available in the smaller firm – but which, perhaps surprisingly, is often not, or not to the same stimulating degree, in the larger ones – is the sheer excitement of executive decision-making. At the top of a large company it can become dull, dreary and rather routine, as the directors indeed know more and more about less and less – whether due to IT (unlikely in their case) or not.

Moreover, it becomes difficult to make an impact with a large company. Alas for the person in the larger organisation who strives to reach the main board, and then finds that the air and the view are disappointing! Meanwhile, he has not seen his children grow up, his wife by then will have established her own separate, much coveted existence and within a year or two of reaching the top, the company is taken over, the company name changed, and nobody remembers either him or the original firm. Worse still, while at the top of the larger organisation, both before and possibly after the takeover, even if he survives, most of his friends are not interested and his wife is the least impressed of them all.

Also, it is much easier to motivate few people than many. There is an in-built advantage, even charm, in supervising 5000 people compared with 20 000. The trigger point when sheer numbers become counterproductive is remarkably low; a company can lose control surprisingly quickly. It is rather similar to a teacher. If teaching 20 people, he will know all their names; if teaching 25 he will probably not know any! (There are some, of course, and they constitute a large minority, who take special pride in working for the larger organisations. They like to work for successful companies and ones that others have heard of.)

MAKING THE TRANSITION

The seemingly effortless transition from the big corporate to the SME can be disrupted by the fact that in one crucial area, at least, the experience gained in the former will be less comprehensive than that gained in SMEs. The big, all-encompassing firms – because of their very structures and sophistication, which usually offer the individual a better foundation for business life – do not prepare the individual for the legal aspects of corporate life. In the bigger firms, somebody else caters for this increasingly cumbersome and onerous aspect of contemporary business.

At the smaller company, the director will have to tackle all the legal aspects independently and quickly. It can prove exacting and unexpectedly demanding. Be that as it may, the bigger firms should still be a chosen path to preparing for a career in the smaller firms. Indeed, it does not really work the other way around. Family firms, especially, but also smaller ones generally, if they are to flourish, are tightly controlled and managed from the top, leaving little room for personal development. If it is small, with perhaps £100 million turnover per annum, a company will often fall to around £50 million rather than rise to £150 million, illustrating yet again the vulnerable nature of these types of companies.

Unfortunately, the smaller company – and even the private firm, and unlike the situation pertaining to the plc – often needs to diversify in order to spread risk. As this is the opposite of what is usually, and rightly, advocated for the disciplined running of a plc, it highlights all too starkly that a director familiar with one situation should not assume he understands the other. Admittedly, some will refute this, arguing that it is the same in both situations, and that the smaller company would not have the people to handle a big diversification!

If the smaller firm succeeds in growing, and so graduates from being a smaller concern, partly perhaps to avoid being gobbled up, it enters a new domain which can seem to be a foreign country. Some staff will fail to adjust and develop accordingly; others will relish the challenge. If the smaller firm fails, it can be a question of not making the transition from founder to manager.

Again, unlike the plc or indeed unlike large companies generally, the smaller company, whether private or not, cannot afford to pay large numbers of directors large amounts of salary. They simply have not got the resources to do so, except in the most unusual circumstances – perhaps where they are truly dominant and can consequently dictate the margins in their niche of their sector. The smaller company, therefore, in consequence, needs to employ a few very able directors for whom they will need to pay the top rates and can afford to do so. This discipline, even when recognised by the smaller company, can put it at a disadvantage; their larger brethren will be recruiting and possibly retaining a strong, able, balanced and well-paid team at the top.

The IT revolution is also a mixed blessing to the smaller company. It is now possible to buy procedures, much of the know-how, off the shelf, instantly. Alas, so can the competition and with IT comes the downside – a propensity to acquire too much detail and thus make it harder to see the full picture. We are becoming a business fraternity which is expert in fewer areas and consequently less able to see the whole picture. At main board level, the broad canvas should be the name of the game. However, treated with care and caution, IT has helped to make smaller firms viable, fashionable and easier to establish.

As the smaller company succeeds and grows, not only are its structures growing but also it becomes more capital-intensive and so a harder place in which to make changes. Why does that not make the smaller firm less attractive to directors? Because most people involved in them simply do not appreciate that this is the case.

There is a difference between large and smaller companies when downsizing as well. In the case of larger groups, savings are usually left to the corporate headquarters – a distant, grey, impersonal organisation. In the case of smaller firms, however, it tends to be that each site plays a more direct and crucial role.

Or again, in the smaller company all sorts of other problems are there or building up or will do so shortly, but the directors are blindly, conveniently and temporarily unaffected by them. Many of this group do not have sufficient grasp of the basics of their company, of how a company works. They have not started in the bigger firm nor do they have around them effective, relevant NEDs who will act as confidants, outsiders with an insider feel, people who, with no career in the firm and possibly little direct financial interest either, remain truly independent. (If the company cannot recognise that they are receiving such a valued input from their NEDs, then they should change them.) It is easy to assume that the NED plays a minimal or much diminished role with such companies, that traditionally they are associated with larger firms and even plcs. This is no longer remotely the case. Some directors cannot answer basic questions such as, "How much money is in the bank?" or "What is the total pay bill?"

It is manifestly even worse than that in companies which operate in "young" sectors such as PR, the media and IT. Here there is a genuine buzz about what they do, a passion and loyalty, a feeling of a team of individuals who gain job satisfaction in abundance. What they cannot see – because they are not looking, and they are not looking because they did not know that they should, and this, in turn, is because the board is equally ignorant – is that in order to survive a company usually needs to make a profit, and that is even before looking at the more fundamental cash flow figures. It is simply not good enough to be up all night on some creative exercise which will make a loss for the firm the next morning. In short, many of the companies who operate in the Soho Village are rather naive, corporately, and the sophisticated business person should join them only after thorough due diligence. The fun, enthusiasm and sheer buzz of such companies is no substitute for caution and a jaundiced view of the firm's longer-term business viability.

Furthermore, there is another perfidious element which should make the smaller firm less attractive, but does not. In small companies there is little incentive for the board – who are hands-on directors, owners, founders, possibly first-generation to boot – to delegate. By not doing so, they demotivate the keen employees who have probably joined originally because they "share the vision" but subsequently do not develop as individuals. It also means that the directors are more likely to make mistakes, especially as the firm grows, and as its needs change. Despite change, there will be little awareness of the need for fresh approaches, and new colleagues. The director who proved against the odds that the company could make it, who persuaded a reluctant bank manager, is not a natural to listen and oblige. That is so unless he is exceptional, has no choice or has, more positively, an NED who can communicate the message effectively – which means, in most cases, having the right chemistry. They have survived, more often than not, because in some form or other and after some rough rides and steep acrimonious learning curves, they have acquired the right team of NEDs.

What will be "right" about these NEDs? It mainly depends on whether they are operating within a public or a family firm. The common characteristics, however, are that they understand the mentality of those running a smaller enterprise – their fears and aspirations, dreams and limitations. If the company is growing they will not prevent things happening, but channel entrepreneurialism rather than stifle it. They will understand that fixed costs rise with growth – it is one of the growing pains of a successful company, but many small companies simply do not appreciate this. However, there are many disadvantages in working for the smaller firm. Many smaller companies do not understand this and the process is even more worrying and painful than perhaps it need be. The NEDs are there, not as company doctors, but as the people who ease the corporate pain at this stage in their journey.

Indeed, one of the best services an NED can make is to highlight for his younger or less-experienced board colleagues that in the early years of an SME it is important to sacrifice profit for growth – and to make decisions relatively quickly. To achieve that, the NED will rely heavily on the chemistry between him and his board colleagues!

In addition, perhaps the NED will have come from a larger company and will have seen all these stages before. He will be reassuring, showing what is cruel necessity and what is priority, and reminding his colleagues that they are not the first company to be facing these challenges.

RELATIONSHIPS

The relationship between big firms and small ones is another labyrinth. It is an unbalanced and unhelpful one, with the guilty finger pointing mainly at the larger firm. Bigger companies often do not make much effort to understand the smaller company; if they have a smaller company within their ranks, they sometimes do not concentrate sufficiently to agree to sell it, which could be the answer, simply because it is merely a small part of the group. The deal will mean little to the parent but a lot to the smaller one (occasionally, there is an opportunity here; if it means so little to the parent, then the parent might not be that interested in it and may be willing to get rid of it – so a bargain could be in the offing). There is, of course, also the law of the jungle. The wise mouse keeps out of the way of the lion. And the trend is also moving in favour of greater focus when selling companies, regardless of their size. With the introduction of value management, the theme today in the bigger companies is to concentrate on core activities. The non-core ones will appear on the company's corporate radar as being just that, adversely effecting their capital employed in that profit centre.

The large companies tend to be paid quicker than do the smaller ones. Both need the discipline of early or reasonable payment but, again, the smaller company has less resources and fat to fall back on. Its need is more crucial. Borrowing is not an option for the smaller company – not because the law precludes it, but because more often than not, there is no culture of borrowing.

If a bigger company chooses to buy a smaller one, surprisingly, it often tends to leave it to middle management to run it. This is rather odd and short-sighted because the firm will have been bought either because the new parent company has a fascination towards it; or believes, possibly erroneously, that it is a jewel, a building block in the corporate edifice; or expects it to facilitate access to a niche market. Why should middle management suddenly and peculiarly be qualified to run this and yet not their own company? A smaller company, previously separate from the new parent – with a different culture, with an unproven track record in the new grouping, with staff who did not expect to see their careers cur-tailed or put on a different plateau – will need plenty of direction. So leave it all to middle management! Why? Integration of a smaller company is crucial, critical and often rather demanding. That is why the acquisition often fails in practice. The initial exercises, logic and due diligence might be completed satisfactorily but the subsequent integration might be carelessly executed. Today, companies are having to pay even higher prices for other companies and as the margins are less, making the integration even more important.

There is a propensity, especially prevalent among smaller companies and when conducting business with larger or more established ones, to be prepared to work at a loss in the hope of securing the business and then converting it to profitability at a later date. This may be valid 1 per cent of the time, but no more frequently than that. Usually neither goodwill nor future business follows. Instead, the company has been used and misused, and hopes have been raised merely to have them dashed; valuable time has been wasted, which cannot be afforded.

Ever since governments chose or were expected to be involved directly in setting the atmosphere and even the rules for business, the temptation to add further red tape has become irresistible. In opposition, it is one of the safest, most popular, clarion cries – "We will cut red tape, especially as it effects the SME – our future lies with them, etc." Nothing new in the message, nothing usually new in the subsequent government action either. Red tape is growing and small companies tend not to be able to cope with it.

Finally, medium-sized companies have two distinct advantages over their even smaller brethren. They have more of the tools, the levers, for operating the company even if they do not necessarily appreciate that they have them or know how to use them. Sometimes there is so much cumbersome dead wood in the organisation that they are unaware of the advantages they possess.

Again, the medium-sized company has the benefit over its smaller counterpart of the knowledge which it will have accrued from merely surviving and growing to that larger size. It has at least reached the next stage on the corporate evolutionary scale. Each step up can be very emotional. Each of the four categories of company being considered in this chapter – the smaller firm, its private counterpart, the medium-sized organisations and the larger ones – face special problems which go hand-in-hand with their respective benefits. For the medium-sized company, their very size – not too big, not too small, possibly not too naive either – will, by definition, become attractive to a takeover. They have put their corporate heads above the parapet.

If the director is with a family firm, he will have other challenges. He may also have those of managing growth – but it is less likely. Rather it is a matter of recognising his role vis-à-vis the family, appreciating what the family will allow him to do by necessity, or by choice or, better, they will understand his rights. Either way, it requires tact on behalf of the NED and awareness by the family.

The cardinal test for the NED, the non-family member of the board, is to have helped bring about necessary change with no blood on the boardroom floor and in a way in which it is impossible to ascribe blame to any member of the family. Change in this context is not confined to structural or personnel; it could just as well be a matter of tidying up the customer base. A long-established, much-cherished, loyally cultivated and retained client might be worth losing. It could be costing the family firm more than it is worth. The family firm can afford to lose that account and the external director is there to say so and suggest that the family firm moves on.

In a way, the family firm is the most wonderful model if it works correctly and remains loyal to its original concept. It will need to exceed, be better than its equivalent plc, in order to avoid the temptation to float. Indeed, the concept behind family firms is excellent; they usually look after their staff especially well. If they know their industry and in the absence of Stock Exchange pressures, and if they do not go asleep, either for a financial year or for a generation, they should, and could, do very well. As for the family, the accumulated wealth, residual in the firm, qualifies as an uncommonly tax-efficient vehicle. If the family needs or wishes to "cash in", the members may benefit from a windfall, but who then looks after that? And where can it be placed or how can it be managed in a way equal or better than the means previously existing in the former family firm structure?

Any company with a narrow business stream, such as an IT company, should think very carefully about going public. Such a business lacks flexibility, and will be prone to issuing profit warnings – a cardinal sin. A logical plc needs a certain degree of robustness.

THE PSYCHOLOGY OF THE SHARE PRICE

Some directors feel much more comfortable in the private sector. (If the company is a plc and it has a small market cap, it may be best to take it private – delist from the Stock Exchange – or break the company up). For example, one of the overriding and determining factors in a plc is sentiment. Plcs are driven more by that than by reality, and yet reality is about being mindful of how sentiment can drive a share price. And to a plc, share price is, of course, one of the *raisons d'être* of their very existence! In a private company, the directors can concentrate on the operations of the business, not on the sentiment. The NED, incidentally, can, should and is best qualified of all at board level to hover over both – operations and sentiment – bringing a balance and relationship between the two.

One can learn a great deal about the maturity of a director, or a whole board, by how they react to their company's share price. Directors become overwrought because they look at the share price on too short a perspective. Most of them look at the price daily, and more remuneration packages nowadays are being based on the upward movement of the share price. Instead, directors should concentrate on managing their companies in the best possible way and for long-term growth.

There is not only an art in reviewing the share price; there is genuine skill in ensuring that it is likely to show achievable and sustained upward movement. If a company makes a mistake, buys the wrong company, it is better to acknowledge that fact speedily by selling that company. However, by selling, the share price will probably be adversely affected; hence the reason why many directors do not sell, thereby avoiding taking the right action because of sentiment.

By taking a longer view, the company will want to clear the slate. Boards cannot prop up sentiment artificially! Rather it has to be based on real performance and proper foundations; not via smoke and mirrors assisted by clever presentations and by avoiding taking difficult decisions. Take heart; share prices do not matter as much as "Are you on the right track for the future?"

And remember, share movements are often exaggerated – rising too high and falling too low, and the steeper they rise the sharper they fall. Do not complain unduly about your share price, or regard a perceived unfairness as a reason to go private. The market can be wrong and, if it is, take advantage and snap up a bundle of the shares at a discount. Remember too that if the fundamentals are sound it is rather helpful to have an artificially low share price! The City's view of the share price has been discussed in Chapter 3.

It is a good discipline for a private company to behave as if it is a plc, ensuring that the management accounts are out on time and the year-end accounts completed quickly.

Of course, one of the primary reasons for converting a private firm into a plc is to raise capital. Perhaps, therefore, the halcyon situation in corporate life is to be a private firm which is of a certain size and is able to raise capital without going public.

PASSION AND SENTIMENT

Many family firms feel undervalued and misunderstood. (This is sad and somewhat odd; in the USA and especially in Italy, employees are often very proud indeed to be in a family firm.) Emotional issues can predominate, and family firms often actually fail because of this. The NED first must, therefore, deal with the family issues; unless he resolves or accommodates those he cannot deal with the business ones, nor will there be a business in the foreseeable future. It is inordinately easy to create disharmony and split the family asunder, which inevitably leads to catastrophic corporate consequences.

The causes of the emotion can change as the family changes, and they change as the founding generation ages and the company matures. Crucially, the NED needs to help the founding generation find a suitable exit. Most do not, and the majority of family firms either have no inclination or desire to do so until it is woefully late. By exit, the family will mean receiving an effective financial package and the only telling package is the one whose roots and foundations were prepared at least a decade previously. The exit cannot be concocted overnight, in panic and under the suspicious gaze of the succeeding generation. At the best of times, family members can fall out and it is usually over money. Usually, the second generation is more willing to retire than are the founders. The original generation are special, are unique and need to be treated as such.

What is almost as important as managing the eventual exit is the family firm's relationship with their banks. The role of their banks can be to make or break and so much so that every family board member should have the two words "Exit" and "Bank" on their desks as a persistent, gentle reminder. Moreover, it is somewhat of a red herring to focus too much on "the family" per se. Sometimes family influence is good, sometimes it is not – just like the relative merits of the input of management generally.

Some would argue, however, that in many cases family members do not feel either undervalued or misunderstood and they are not bothered either way. The family does bother from one perspective; if it sells out, the family knows it would find it inordinately difficult to walk around their home town where their former employees live. However hard the family fought a hostile takeover, the local walk will still be an awkward one. The sale will have disestablished a hitherto ordered relationship. In a family firm, staff know their place and if they are paid a lower rate – which is not necessarily always the case – they know that the family will look after them. The sale destroys all that.

So much of the wealth of the family firm is tied up in the firm. Its ultimate durability is its ability to adapt and appoint the relevant member of the family. That equals succession planning, and succession planning can happen only if the exit and financial packages are in place, and recognised as being fair to the rest of the family.

It is wise to plan an exit even if there is no intention of giving up. At least then there will be a strategy in place, in reserve, in case there is a sudden offer. Remember that the majority of firms survive independently for less than 30 years, and in that majority are a huge percentage that survive independently for only ten years or less.

There are different dynamisms in family firms and plcs. Different timescales for strategy initiatives, different risk profiles, different appetites for debt restructuring. Even the financial needs and objectives of the wider family, due to personal tax planning implications, are all different. So despite the similarities, the characteristics and the ability of one to become the other it is, in reality, almost a miracle that a company can grow or develop or change its corporate status in this way.

Remember, too, that if the director is also the founder and he sees his company grow, it is rather like a father seeing his child grow. He will need to learn to let go, which means succession planning. It is a very difficult challenge; the firm will have its DNA, its character, and yet the firm will be developing its own separate identity as well.

Too many families – despite their undoubted affection for, and sense of responsibility to, their employees, the staff – can nevertheless behave as if only the family really matters. They would not recognise this. Indeed because it strikes at the heart of their corporate philosophy – and remember they will have been brought up, bred for the purple, with a much longer apprenticeship than most to run the firm – it is surprising that they are usually worse than others. And it is not only the staff who worry about succession, so do the firm's customers as well.

There is an additional factor to consider. If the main family member is wealthy, independent and still in charge of the company, he will have an emotional attachment to it but will not be dependent upon its commercial success in the same way as others. This is the worse possible combination!

It is a pivotal responsibility, therefore, to achieve a smooth succession. But should the successor invariably be a member of the family? History rather cautions against it. Few family firms survive into the second generation. It can be a question of from rags to riches and back again within three generations. In fact, many family businesses do not really fail, even after two generations. They are taken over and the business carries on as such with the subtle difference; they have lost the special factor which made them unique in the first place. It will have gone for good and probably the new owner will have purchased a concept which has either lost its original momentum or, at least, was acquired at an inflated price. (The third generation is "always" for sale, is a general maxim. But it need not be so. The usual reason for the predictable finite life of the family firm is the propensity to squabble among the members of the family of that generation.)

A main board role for an outsider in a family firm is one of the hardest corporate challenges. There can be disputes between family members. Female members – still – can be excluded and feel strongly that this is both unfair and short-sighted; the family will have a tradition of conducting their affairs in a rather rigid manner. To take a vote at a family board meeting is a bold, unfamiliar event and should be considered only as a last resort. And what should your attitude be towards other, non-family members? After all, it can be acutely demotivating to exclude non-family members and equally demotivating to be competent, be non-family and have to tolerate mediocrity above you, especially when you have chosen the special atmosphere of the family firm in the first place.

FURTHER COMPLICATIONS AND BENEFITS

Can a non-family member not be on the board but hold equity? Usually not. If someone outside the family does hold shares, all concerned need to be aware that disgruntled members of the family might try to use such a person as a tool – which needs to be prevented. Meanwhile, there remains a loyal staff and mounting competition outside. It can be very demotivating if only the family can hold equity! At least one rule is clear – though often ignored – never be a minority shareholder in a private firm. You will have no responsibilities and no rights, merely be leaving your money at the beck and call of a third party over whom you have no influence.

In addition, the disadvantage of a family firm – and a characteristic shared by all small firms – is that they, above all, can ill afford to make mistakes. They have no fat, no hidden or reserve resources on which to fall back. And yet, smaller firms share many similar problems to their larger counterparts and do not have the time, flexibility and leeway to accommodate them. Finally, it is a wise precaution, whether a family member or not – and especially if not – never to take a family firm's views at face value!

Then there is the smaller firm which is neither the family nor the public version, it is the stand-alone subsidiary of a larger group. This is the junior, least satisfying variety. However large, impressive or even distinctive, it is a subsidiary and the buck does not stop at its board. It can be bigger than many independent companies, but it remains a small entity – in this case, a minority part of the larger corporate group. To complicate the situation somewhat, a few of these subsidiaries are almost truly independent! But the litmus test still applies – the buck does not stop with them; the budget is decided elsewhere, at the main board.

Family businesses and smaller firms generally – even stand-alone subsidiaries – all have a key role to play in corporate life. They are to be treated with respect; most outperform quoted companies by up to 40 per cent, over a period of 20 years! And the reason is simple – the best ones tend to have commitment from their team, in a way which many larger companies fail to establish or maintain.

They face a legion of challenges, to a degree that larger ones do not. Yet the smaller companies are a piece – perhaps one of the cornerstones – of the wider corporate scene. They are vehicles for entrepreneurs and they can be the powerhouse of corporate activity. They are not to be ignored, nor penalised and above all not to be ridiculed.

6
THE GLASS CEILING

It would be easy to conclude that, with so few women on Britain's main boards – despite half the graduates over the last two decades being female – this chapter should be superficial and shallow. This would be totally wrong and rash; top business women may be few in number but those who have ascended the corporate peak fall into two separate and interesting categories, while the proverbial glass ceiling, which has prevented others from arriving, is already cracking. Indeed, it could and should smash sooner than most males or females think.

TWO GROUPS, TWO ROUTES

The first group, the obvious one, comprises those who owe their original position largely to who they are. Their original legitimacy was debateable even if, in certain cases, their subsequent performance has been effective. Until recently, this group constituted almost the only way of ascending to the boardroom. The corollary is that most currently *in situ* are of the older generation, business-wise, usually 53-plus or so. Sometimes, effortlessly or via great perseverance, they either forget completely that they have never graduated through the ranks of corporate Britain or behave as if they have forgotten. However capable they become, this cadre have, nevertheless, been deprived of the inescapable advantage that a career in business offers anybody – male or female – at board level.

Not to experience the lowly positions, the frustrations, the lack of any guarantee of ever reaching the main board even if they want to, is to miss more than a trick or two. And it shows. Fascinatingly, this deprivation is rather more evident to their male colleagues than the women often realise. The reasons for the reluctance from their male counterparts to convey their true feelings is due either to their being too polite or being too sheepish.

Some women in this group, despite their poise and apparent success, seem to operate at only one level of understanding. The giveaway is their posing of an intelligent question, which, at the time, might appear to be both a productive and positive contribu-tion but which, subsequently, is shown to have little or no link to the discussion that either proceeded or followed. Rather, it is an isolated contribution gleaned from another source or forum; pos-sibly, if they are a successful gatherer of other NED positions, from another board on which they sit. At least this group does not suffer, though, from the lack of self-confidence which still plagues many women of their generation or even of the one which succeeds them.

Of course, all but a bigot or corporate chauvinist will lament this paucity of women at board level. Most of the reasons for their continued absence are crassly obvious and have been rehearsed routinely on paper and within companies. However, the situation remains stark. There are currently around 1200 directors (executive and NED) in the FTSE 100, 70 of whom are women. There are fewer than ten female executive directors in the FTSE 100.

It is the other group, those who come through the ranks, who are altogether more interesting even if, due to their numerical inferiority, they have less immediate impact. The future female contribution will be via them; they are the Young Turks to the old guard. Those of them already at the top, against the odds, have gained the prize against their male counterparts and they are irritated beyond belief that their success should be questioned or should still warrant much discussion or profiling.

However, for the majority of able career women who are still just below the main board there is a glass ceiling which they have not passed through, but can easily detect. Many also believe that they might never do so and yet feel that this would be grossly unfair. Also, being glass, it allows them temptingly to see what might be.

ADVANTAGES AND DISADVANTAGES

So what is stopping them? There are many dotty reasons given, from "The behaviour of men and women in the workplace can be traced back to puberty" to "Many men feel nervous with the new presence of career women and about breaking rules of conformity to male groups", or "Women approach their relationships with their male bosses as a means of replacing the closeness with their fathers that was lost when they went through puberty." All entertaining thoughts, some of which might be regarded as significant. But they do not advance women's careers greatly nor will they convince their male counterparts who, rightly or wrongly, sit in most seats of corporate power.

It is necessary to reflect for a moment on some of the possible or more circumspect psychological reasons put forward by both men and, more importantly, by women themselves. Many boys' games encourage competitiveness and aggression, and business has been run by men for so long that companies have strong male character- istics. Women have different leadership styles from men. Even today, with the lamentable figures highlighted above, it is clear to all but the most prejudiced and intolerant that women desire to build the right team, to avoid company politics, to encourage open discussion and to be tough in a pleasant, constructive way. In the process, they judge their effectiveness on how much loyalty they have generated and can rely upon. Most women, however, remain "non-confrontational" and this limits their chances of competing effectively.

If the best companies gain most from their top team by treating them as individuals, and if that is where motivation is paramount, then women have the better set of attributes, naturally available, there to be developed but unfortunately often discarded, ignored or wasted by corporate Britain.

Perhaps it is little surprise, therefore, that where women have already succeeded in larger numbers, such as in the infamous dot.com companies or media and PR firms, they are in sectors which discourage hierarchies. It does not follow that because the dot.coms usually failed, possibly largely because of poor manage- ment rather than lack of money, that women are to have a black mark against their boardroom capabilities.

If women do not want to, or cannot, behave like their male counterparts and will not blow their own trumpets, are they flawed and ultimately condemned? Surely not, for the trend is, once more, moving in their direction. There is a new generation of women growing up who believe that they can and should be as successful as men. Any director with a daughter who is at university or has graduated will know this and will want to see his daughter succeed. He will not want to put barriers in her way, especially if they are barriers of structure and hierarchy which can be dismantled and are currently being maintained largely by him! The younger women have a different set of expectations from the generation and a half above them; they expect equality and they will not have the tolerance towards discrimination that their predecessors displayed.

There are signs aplenty for those bothered and willing to look. Look no further than the plight of local political associations. In the past such bodies were one of the few outlets for those women who wished to have influence on the broader scale. Now with other, more conventional business openings available, albeit largely at the lower rungs of the ladder, most political associations do not attract women aged below 40.

WHAT THE WOMEN CAN DO

Women, though, can be their own worst enemies. The group at the top, referred to at the beginning of this chapter, with no career experience through the corporate ranks, can with some exceptions make the wrong noises, make it clear that they have arrived and adopt a chippy, unhelpful attitude. And then the career women of the next generation may compound the problem by underselling themselves. The latter are often poor negotiators when it comes to terms and conditions, comparing those conditions with other women rather than, justifiably, with their potential male counterparts. It becomes a vicious circle to the ultimate detriment of all. (The gulf between men's and women's pay increases at executive levels! In the USA, Fortune 500 companies' women are paid about 70 per cent of the men's rate at that level – especially depressing when the USA enjoys more women in higher positions than does the UK.)

Women can also fail to reach the boardroom because they give up the race. They might not choose to further their careers. Of course, some stop to have a family, others complain loudly and frequently that it is grossly unfair that they have the baby, while others still have their babies and hire a nanny, returning to their careers with haste. Others find the competitive environment not to be for them, and it could become even less attractive to them if, as is likely, they have married or have a partner who is educated or successful or preferably both. Others succumb to the almost unconscious undercurrents which together can exert a great psychological barrier to furthering their business careers. Even little points can do this, such as their husbands not wanting them to be on the telephone making business calls for a large proportion of the evening.

Again, however, the trend is moving steadily in favour of women. Increasing numbers of men leave because they reach a certain level, or feel content and retire early to enjoy opportunities not available to any previous generation. The best companies are increasingly recognising the need to develop structures which reflect this trend, by offering opportunities to part-timers and recognising the necessity to balance work/family needs.

IN TIME, MUCH COULD CHANGE

Many companies, though, do not encourage part-timers – whether male or female, principally the latter – and so they are wasted.

Fortunately, again the trend is changing – a breeze is blowing in their favour. Part-timers are loyal and grateful and display the "three-day-week" scenario of putting in four days' work in a mere three days. If they are potential part-timers they might be former employees and will be known already by the company, so there is even less excuse for their former employee not to re-engage them. Nor should their new status debar them from the boardroom, at least as an NED.

The original group of women NEDs, those with no previous corporate career, are even more part-time, but it has not prevented them from being acceptable to their male counterparts.

There are already possibly sufficient numbers of career women at the top or just below, offering the proof that they do not need to act like men in order to get to the top. They are in the driving seat and are setting the pace. Alas, occasionally, women discriminate against women! And then there is discrimination by small men towards tall women – and no doubt in time vice versa as well! Perhaps also some women do not prefer to be managed by women but are happy instead to be managed by men, and possibly men, on the whole, do not mind being managed by women! Thankfully, there are only two sexes, for the combinations are varied enough already.

A host of other reasons can be listed for the small number of women at the top – inadequate child care facilities, the clubbiness of male-dominated boardrooms, inflexible structures, selection procedures, stereotyped assumptions about their ability and character (often enhanced by the media), old boy networks, and their likely inability to be as mobile as their male counterparts (until the children are older at least).

There are also some subtle trends and factors often completely or partially ignored. There are differences in acceptability between regions – women have a harder time in the North and also in the traditional industries. Women often fail to apply for the top positions because they lack confidence – and no procedure or audit can overcome the imbalance if that is the case. Sometimes wives have an intuitive input on whether a female colleague of their husband's is right for promotion and the husband might listen, rightly or wrongly.

Those women who are at the top, whether from groups one or two, share one disadvantage, which can be irksome and even dangerous but which, fortunately, will surely and easily be removed. Remarkably, perhaps, even today with international chains of hotels, most hotels still do not really know how to look after the needs of business women. Women on business may be travelling alone, but they do not want to drink alone at the bar, nor dine alone, nor have a room on the ground floor. They need and should expect the understanding hand of a sensitively run business and be allowed to have the comforts – the gym, better situated rooms, perhaps even a more comprehensive room service – without any of the worries or embarrassments. International hotel chains are missing a trick and a golden opportunity. Within a short period possibly as many as half of all business guests will be women.

So women are rising more rapidly within their organisations, partly due to their own efforts, and are being held back, partly due to their own attitudes. The picture is changing and the pressure for change, generated by a new attitude by a large minority of men and due to the impatience of the younger generation of women, bodes well for corporate UK. The softening of business styles, the seeking of consensus at board level and the dismantling of hierarchies in many industries – to say nothing of the proliferation of smaller

companies which women can establish, control and excel in – all
mitigate well for half the employable population (a figure steadily
balancing in favour of women), who are more than half of the
consumers purchasing the products and services of the majority of
our businesses.

7
CORPORATE CHARACTERS AND CULTURES

Companies have an entity beyond their mere existence. They each have a chemistry, style and tradition, which should be acknowledged, often enhanced, sometimes challenged but never ignored.

The director can join the board and hope to influence one or other of these factors. He would be unwise; the challenge may prove too great or not worth the effort or be both counter-productive and destructive. Better to join in order to develop via a healthy respect for what exists already.

GETTING THEIR ACTS TOGETHER

Crucially the company needs to understand at main board level and beyond any ambiguity, what it stands for. Otherwise, two imme-diate problems arise: first, those below the main board will have an even hazier idea and so cannot possibly operate as part of a successful team and, second, the company will attract those with the wrong set of skills. Together, they combine to ruin the best recipe.

For instance, it may be that the board does not even believe that the company has a right to survive! In fact, sometimes what appears to be an august array of distinguished directors is little more than a loose gathering of diverse corporate characters. Some companies do not have an inner conviction; they merely enthuse in a rather haphazard way. In such cases, it is better if the directors give their company a corporate makeover and, with its best face showing, try to sell it to a board which possesses the missing ingredients. Or again, if the board has no meaningful strategy, it might as well put a "for sale" sign up; if the board does not reflect the perceived strategy, the company is in equal trouble. It is also unbelievable how much time some companies spend composing their corporate mission statements, as if the words alone are sufficient.

What are the values the company stands for – integrity, to be world-class, to outperform all others? What does it mean by such bland words? And there are a further dozen equally banal words for each one of these. There is no point in giving all employees a rule book or an extensive induction when there is not a consensus or when the rule book does not reflect the culture. How else can the staff treat the customer appropriately or the engineer tackle the problem at 4am when there is nobody else around to ask? (In practice, companies tend to operate one of two philosophies – either have a rule book for everything or give considerable freedom.)

Moreover, too often directors assume that their peers, or those below, will ask if they do not understand an instruction or a point.

Usually this is not the case. There is an art, taught by no business school, of being able to check without appearing to meddle. Some directors can even play a game – regularly checking up on small matters, which are usually easy to determine and thereby give the impression that they are watching the bigger issues as well. Directors need to ask the single question, "What do people actually do?" Daft? Then why is it that so many directors do not know!

The "below board level" perceptions constitute a fascinating and fundamental area for the board. The board and the rest of the organisation are in reality two entities with different cultures and yet each are irrevocably linked and dependent upon each other. If the board conveys even a hint of not being clear and aware of its goals, no strategy will or can work – nor does it deserve to. If it is a confused board it is a confused company. Those below will not be in a position to challenge, because they will not know what the board wants; they will be unaware of the company's culture.

In practice, it is not quite so stark as that; boards are collegiate and succession planning stops at board level. Below that, the company is more structured and structured organisations do not encourage a culture which is a challenging one by nature. However, they still legitimately expect a clear lead from the board above them.

Fortunately, matters are improving as UK industry generally becomes more effective, with all levels increasingly understanding each other, helped in this instance by a reduction in the number of layers of management. Indeed, the process of de-layering has become so well established that there is a real danger that it might go too far. In so doing inefficiencies will re-establish themselves and the original, supposedly daft question will go to the top of the agenda again.

Frequently, companies fail to prepare their teams for the times which will pose new challenges, requiring different skills. Preparing for the so-called unexpected without being overcautious is a difficult compromise to achieve. For instance, the end of a period of growth, whether for the company or across the economy as a whole, creates fundamental problems for directors. The previous period will have helped establish an ethos of overconfidence while at the same time creating a team which will be inexperienced in the other stages of the economic cycle. When there is a downturn, or a pause in the growth story, near panic sets in when a reflective period would suffice in order to keep the board steady and relevant in its pursuit of a legitimate strategy. In extreme cases, a dip in profits, while still leaving a healthy overall performance, can turn the younger director pale and make his colleagues panic.

The type of company least proficient in predicting trends and having the commensurate skills tends to be one where an entrepreneur plays or has played a cardinal role in the company. The process of establishing processes, of making the steps from self-centred entrepreneur to organised, conventional structures, simply has not been allowed to develop; and the successful establishing of relevant processes is a right step in the direction of establishing the company's culture.

In practice, these self-same companies tend to be the smaller firms. Such organisations often do not even attempt to progress along these necessary steps, let alone reach a satisfactory conclusion. Step one: the entrepreneur is all-powerful, owns the equity, owns the ideas and is used to leading the decision-making process. There are no layers between him and action. He says and it is done. The entire organisation relies on his moods and sure touch. If matters go wrong, the staff rely on him to put it right. This is not a pleasant stage or scenario for his staff. He puts uncultured, untutored pressure on the level below and the lines are short.

Two factors make a sad situation awful. The company has a *raison d'être* to exist but there is an inevitability of what will happen next, because the company has not reached the second step. And the true picture is further disguised, in the short term at least, because such companies are usually in a period of growth and all looks healthy. The company needs to put the structures and processes in place and quickly.

Then there is accountability. The strategy will have a common parentage and the company culture will exist and be shared. More staff will be involved. If the board then recruits externally, which it possibly should by then, it is important that the new directors are committed to the new culture and strategy they buy into.

The entrepreneur will not comply meekly. He will dislike structures. No longer will a meeting take place when he arrives sometime on Monday morning, having just flown in from the south of Spain. No longer will he be able to say, "We will have a meeting tomorrow." The management meetings will be set, there will be a cycle and he will attend them on the agreed date and listen to colleagues; otherwise, there is still no staff commitment, no company structure and the company remains as vulnerable as before.

The final step is a permanent change of attitude, of character, in the entrepreneur. No longer is it a question of him having the ideas and then browbeating the nearest colleague to deliver. Rather, it is now a sophisticated exercise to determine who is best to execute what, and how the entrepreneur can help achieve those agreed, collegiate board decisions. It requires more trust all round.

By this stage, the entrepreneur is likely to be bereft. There is no more self-centred excitement emanating from his deal-driven corporate style. The early excitement will have gone, substituted by boring – at least to him – structures and processes; the very conventional structures he probably escaped from in order to set up his own company.

Entrepreneurs make CEOs of conventional companies seem easy to handle. The former create both jobs and companies, develop concepts, have courage and, above all, tenacity. What they lack is the ability to tackle detail. It takes a sensitive director to be able to harness such a volatile and contradictory package.

DISCUSSION, NOT PRESENTATION

The best bosses are prepared to encourage difficult discussions, looking at real issues and threats on the horizon or within the company – and a good board will address these issues. Every company has its sacred cows but good companies will put them to one side. Alas, many companies like and feel more comfortable reliving past battles, trying to make the past better rather than predicting and controlling the future.

With entrepreneurs, a board can easily become swamped with ideas. The directors will need – however difficult in practice – to get the entrepreneur to become his own check and balance. If the restraint is external, the entrepreneur becomes annoyed and, like Toad in *The Wind in the Willows*, will be out on the open road again the moment backs are turned. There is a need – an incredibly difficult corporate challenge – to build the right team around him who can put substance to raw ideas and help the entrepreneur make it all happen. Just a modicom of pressure the wrong way, and all can be lost.

The corporate world falls rather neatly into three: the entre-preneurs (few in number), the mechanics (also few in number), and the controllers (many). The mechanics have no egos, no personal agendas; they understand the business and its culture, and have little ambition beyond doing the best for the entrepreneur. It is a kind of idol worship, healthy in its way, as long as the mechanics are not in thrall to their boss. An effective entrepreneur is only as good as his mechanics. The latter need to hold the mirror up for the entrepreneur to see when an idea is unrealistic – the mirror becomes part of his own checks and balances. Management is all about bribery and kindness.

It is rather frightening, however, whether entrepreneur or not, to contemplate how much good or ill one director can do. He can make or break a company. His contribution, whether positive or negative, can be on a par with the head teacher or the chef; they change and everything seems to change with them.

BOARDS ASSESSING THEMSELVES

In fairness to the entrepreneur, he is not the only type of director in need of a reappraisal of his role. All boards need to reflect and be self-critical, to review themselves. Very few bother. The exercise needs to be conducted with care. It is not a matter of putting the chairman in the dock. The idea is to be positive, to release the corporate energy hitherto stifled at board level. Few conduct the exercise because directors are not conditioned that way. The succession to the board is via a structured career with a slightly political undertone accompanying every step up the ladder. Below board level the structured existence allows people to know where they stand vis-à-vis others. At board level it is all so very, very different. The board operates largely on relationships, which can be hard to read, easy to assume. What really motivates the chairman? What is the real relationship between him and his CEO? There is less certainty about where power lies. The confidence of colleagues might be wafer thin, their real agendas rather different.

The newly promoted director, previously dependent upon a structured environment, will be reluctant to loosen up, speak up, talk openly about colleagues because it is, to him, an unfamiliar situation – and one that can go horribly wrong.

If he is a new appointee, or it is his first main board position, the director will quickly learn another difference between the main board and below; if he enjoyed leading people he will find that desire difficult to satisfy at board level. Main boards do not lead people in the same direct way; they influence and ensure that the building blocks are in place for others to take the direct action. Frequently main board positions can be disappointing; they can lack excitement. Apart from the status and the prospect of being locked up – an increasing prospect despite how few to date have been incarcerated (and those who have gone to jail seem to come out rather quickly and through the front gates) – being on the main board might not prove very exciting after all. Below the board, there are plenty of colleagues and there is a distinctive buzz; it is relatively easy to measure a contribution, to walk around the factory in the evening and actually observe the units made and ready for dispatch, knowing one's own contribution.

On the main board, in contrast, there is a rather unreal air which settles on the agenda. A feeling of debating in a vacuum, of being isolated, of not knowing which decisions will have any measured effect and – even less satisfying if no decision has been made –

merely discussion. Deeper down, the director knows that this is unfair and unrealistic.

We are also back to the structured career below board versus the relationships that sustain a board. Running a division has simple vertical lines of command, people know who should report to whom. On the way up, their only relationship above is with their ultimate boss. It becomes a one-for-one relationship. On the board, it is one for ten or so, and thus there is a need to build lateral relationships.

It is easy to be lost on a board. Both the chairman and the NEDs are there to help – and the CEO should not feel threatened by this approach. NEDs are merely trying to make the CEO and his colleagues more effective members of his executive team.

If the director joins a FTSE 100 company, he will need to want to work within an atmosphere of consensus. In that size of company, consensus by design rather than knockabout will be the style and the expectation, although even that depends somewhat on the style of the chairman.

When self-assessing a board, it is wise to remember a few cardinal points. The agenda needs to be set beforehand, and to be controlled by the chairman – so nobody is allowed to criticise unconstructively or too personally. The topics will be set – they may be mighty and broad such as the agenda of the board, the quality of the decisions, training for the board (corporate governance), the composition of the board (too many/too few NEDs?) succession planning.

If the board feels incapable of assessing itself, independently, it should go for second-best, but it is second-best. It should hire a consultant, an outsider, a catalyst for the debate; who can make unattributable comments, avoiding accusations of personalising the debate.

UNCERTAINTY AND RISK

Consistently, throughout this book, there has been an appeal for directors to dream dreams, to have a vision and to accept challenges but also, as far as possible, to be in control – or as Kipling put it, "If you can dream and not make dreams your master …" To compliment this, it is necessary to be a risk-taker.

There is an understandable aversion to taking risks, encapsulated by the increasing litigious nature of life generally, and corporate life in particular. The Turnbull Report, as part of the series of corporate governance reports, makes risk even more taxing; yet without some risk there will be less profit.

There was an in-built aversion to risk even before the Turnbull Report. In corporate life, nothing can be taken for granted. Difficulties appear as if from nowhere. Yet companies need to take risks and many take too few. Risk is part of the human condition; history is punctuated by it. Columbus took a great risk sailing to America. With risk, of course, some things will go wrong – that is its quality, its very stamp, but it is not all downside. A company – especially one of the bigger ones, can more easily afford to take risks and get some actions wrong; it is the balance between success and failure emanating from taking a calculated risk that matters. A few "local difficulties" are usually acceptable.

Most finance directors are the epitome of risk aversion. They are by nature cautious and their innate caution is nurtured by their training. (At best, there are two types of finance director – the technician and the generalist. The former will remain a finance director, whereas the latter could, if he chose, become a generalist and end up possibly as a CEO. Unfortunately, without experience in diverse corners of more than one company, even the potential generalist with a finance background will remain rather too technically orientated for comfort. For the larger company, the ideal is to have a finance director who is a generalist, and who has, in his team, a tax expert and both a treasurer and a financial controller. The board will be served well, and a future CEO will be in the making, either for that company or for elsewhere.)

Clever directors realise what they are good and bad at, proficient in and ignorant of, what they can do or what is better for others to do instead. They ask what are their company's core and non-core activities and then subcontract out where appropriate. The director needs to know when to refer a matter and when to seize the remit himself and run the company. The decision is not that difficult but arguably only if the director realises that the question needs to be asked in the first place.

Most of us are either pessimists or optimists. There is the pessimism of the intellectual and the optimism of the "I will overcome". A board needs both. Very infrequently are the two characteristics merged effectively in one board member. The finance director tends to be the pessimist, the CEO the optimist. The City sees this division of attitude. They will ask the finance director after the CEO's presentation for "the truth", for the fuller, more rounded picture. But they will also want the CEO to dream; if he is not dreaming, where is the company's vision?

If the company is at the bottom and the director is having a corporate version of a prolapse he might gamble, concluding that he has no further to fall. But the urge to lose the bank's money should not override the more reflective consideration, which should naturally emanate from a conscientious businessman who happens also to be a family man, possibly with children and a mortgage. (Incidentally, if the company is a plc it is, generally, safer never to owe the banks a penny!)

Many companies hit rock bottom because they do not know how to grow, only how to control. The director needs to liberate his colleagues, and the company, from that mindset. (And whatever is the cause of the company's poor performance the director should never resort to advertising, however tempting, as a solution. Such action in such a situation is on a par with taking an aspirin when really the need is to amputate the leg.) Alas, most organisations, even today, are command and control – few are sufficiently confident to encourage much real challenge. Only when times are particularly good will a company allow more than a superficial change of culture. When a wobble returns, the company reverts to type.

There are different types of risk and the safest version – necessary for the person keen to reach the top of the business ladder and then, just as hard, to stay there – is to be prepared to do what others will not do. Often, the successful, when asked how they reached the top, apart from luck and timing, say that they were prepared to do what others dared not attempt; becoming, in the process, the fixer, the useful colleague who makes things happen.

But, alas, there is a snag. A risk is not necessarily greater or lesser depending upon the amount of knowledge available. The army commander might win a battle because of his attention to detail and perhaps even lateral thinking, his daring and cheek, but in business there are other factors which can complicate matters. Directors either have too much or too little data. (Directors must not be afraid to work on a hunch – it might not be so haphazard as it appears. The directors will not be judged on the detail, merely on how the hunch fits the strategy.) There is a trend, as already observed, to have too much because of the ease of access of information in this IT-orientated world. It can be that a director waits too long, as he seeks all the information possible. Better to appreciate that the best operate in a rather different way; they take decisions, often big ones, on very limited data and then have to make it happen. That is homing in on intuition, relying on guts, but is also a simple matter of capitalising on experience. If the director believes that he is 60 per cent or more right to proceed along one route and he feels he has the right people, he should have a go, rather than analyse the issues to death! The simple, golden rule is to develop the capacity for detail without a passion for it. The link between the general view and the detailed one has a further manifestation. A director might preen himself on his ability to understand the business in detail – but that is a chancy criteria to rely upon. Detail is the province of the technician; the director needs to understand how the company is run. The two are not analogous.

Regardless of sector or size of company, directors should cultivate the ability to avoid skating over issues. Probing constantly, the director will have learned to reach conclusions neither too quickly nor too slowly. He will be well rehearsed in the corporate ritual of walking round his desk over and over again, working out the issues before sitting down and deciding. The biggest chance of a mistake being made is when the whole board believes in the decision! The board needs somebody, probably an NED – because it is easier for him, with no career in the company – to maintain the momentum of critical analysis, though without becoming either a bore or an impediment.

Meanwhile, unfortunately, risk aversion is seeping through corporate life. (Partners in professional firms are more reluctant to think laterally on behalf of established clients, for fear of jeopardising the entire partnership.) It is one thing to caution against the temptation to act, but it can, alas, be even more damaging if a director or board is racked with indecision! The risk of inaction can prove worse than action. The balanced assessment firmly grounded on a wide and comprehensive experience, and tested by a team which works as a team, is the catalyst for getting more business decisions right than wrong. In order to achieve the best from the staff, the director will need to teach them to make decisions quickly. In comparison, it is relatively easy to teach a person about the company, its culture and character.

Moreover, the price of failure is getting heavier as change is now increasingly rapid. Just as there is room for the mistake in corporate life (more so if it is your first mistake or the first in that area – repeated mistakes of a similar type are not to be encouraged or endorsed if the director has any instinct for survival, let alone promotion), so there is also room for the gambler who is not an entrepreneur. A useful ploy is to put colleagues at risk but with an invisible and indiscernible safety net. However, failures and mistakes, of course, must never be of sufficient magnitude that the individual or, more critically, the company is allowed to fall too low. And, remember, in the final analysis, failure is often very subjective!

There is a further psychological dimension to failure. An able person will not be attracted to join unless there is a good exit provision. The UK position is auspicious; not through luck but by intention. We practise a more fluid employment policy than those adopted elsewhere within the EU.

METAMORPHOSIS

Clearly, people respond to better management, and to a director who believes in them. But while an individual may be pleasantly surprised by the apparent metamorphosis of his activities, if nurtured, only so much change can take place. People are an awkward asset! Most people can perform above their current expectations but, just as people do not work well if only 70 per cent stretched, nor do they if 110 per cent is asked for. It can be difficult to strike the right balance. It might be one threshold at one time in their lives – perhaps the first time around in a situation, before the novelty wears off or if all is fine on the domestic front – yet lower at other times.

As we progress through an organisation, and get older, or merely change with experience, we need to recognise the psychological processes we pass through. It is hard to be as hungry at 60 as one was at 25, when setting out with a young heart to conquer. If successful, we will not necessarily be so hungry; we can only give so much to our children without spoiling them. When a person is over about 50 and has held top positions, he will want to be more like a statesman, not being up at 5am, attempt to complete a 24-hour working day and acting like a 35-year-old, let alone a 25-year-old. Nothing remotely wrong in that, but the person and his colleagues need to recognise these inevitable and unavoidable facts.

While it is true that after a certain age it is difficult to change, even if willing, there is also the other side to this psychological coin. Directors of a certain age (and others) can listen selectively or cunningly in order to decide whether they can get away with not changing – they practise flummery! Depressingly, most people are conditioned by the age of 30; they know their weaknesses, and may want to find ways of rectifying those shortcomings, but find it inordinately difficult to do so.

When asked to single out the main mistake made in a business life, the majority of directors pick their management of people. What they mean is that they were either too lenient, or too insensitive to the needs of those around them and usually, surprisingly, the former. Constantly, directors hold back in moving colleagues on; they believe with time the person will improve sufficiently when most times he will not. And when he does depart, forceably but belatedly, both he and his previous immediate colleagues will, in all probability, have appreciated the tougher action. It was more obvious to all except the director that something needed to be done, and further postponement merely made it more difficult and costly, both in human and financial terms. Furthermore, if a director does not delegate, he is not doing his job; if he cannot delegate because the colleague is not good enough, then there is no point in employing the colleague. It is not too flippant to say that the majority of business problems are fundamentally caused by people, and that the cures are usually therefore the result of what directors do under this heading. And most directors get the teams they deserve.

However good a colleague might be, if they are not right or good enough, the director must face up to that fact. Of course, there are weak colleagues who can do better, an asset under-utilised, unappreciated by the company and possibly harbouring skills which even the individual does not know are there. Remember, also, that directors will not want to lose their reputations at the end of their careers – they will get their financial reward by then, so why risk it by rocking the boat? It can be restrictive for other directors when a colleague has reached that stage, but better to acknowledge it than ignore it, and attempt to engineer him out of the company a little before that due date. Otherwise the company is doing him more of a favour than vice versa. A director needs to ensure a balance of age and experience around him, not just the young and hungry nor the old and wise, recognising that some people are worn out at 40 and others are still waiting for their first challenge at 60. And then there is the need to have an average age which reflects their clientele or, as the nation becomes older, perhaps there is a legitimate demand for older staff to serve them.

The director could waste less time, avoid frustration and be more successful if he also concentrated on the positives abiding in his staff. Do not spend all the time on the 5 per cent which is poor when 95 per cent might be good.

The advantage of retaining older directors who have seen it all before can be considerable. The downside, though, can be greater if the individuals concerned are holding back the vision of the company as a whole. Again, it is a question of subtle balance. One way of ensuring that the younger directors keep the corporate ship in some sort of equilibrium is to appoint an NED with the experience of different sectors at different times and with the gravitas and broad shoulders which can usually only come with such experience. Otherwise, a new, younger generation of directors recreate the wheel every time the business cycle changes gear. It is all so unnecessary.

(A yardstick of how successful is a director, is his ability to attract top quality, develop them to the full and then see how well they do when they leave. And the process of acquiring the next relevant job can be as much via a chance meeting as a planned one.)

There are people walking around whose abilities have been labelled incorrectly. There are too many leaving school believing that they are successful and others with the label of failure stuck to them. Yet life is a long, unchartered journey, making the original opening up of Africa a Sunday-afternoon stroll. It is interesting to note how many directors in their early forties have never been to university. In their day fewer – too few – went to university, but the best still tended to do so, unless deciding to qualify via a professional firm and miss the graduate route. So what happened? What were the schools assessing which business does not need? Or is there an army of more able people attracted to other walks of life? The brightest at school will subsequently pursue intellectual challenges – and that is not business. Maybe they will go into the professions or academia itself. What are the characteristics which will manifest themselves even at school level and which subsequently will be relevant in business? Tenacity, the ability to take setbacks and bounce back – these are crucial qualities in business, and they are not characteristics which are measured at school level.

We all have setbacks; successful directors are no exception. What is interesting and highly relevant is how they respond to adversity. The best come back even more determined. Entrepreneurial skills are different again; the entrepreneur takes risks, and the school curriculum and routine do not highlight such characteristics.

Unbelievably, or it should be, some directors will still recruit their friends – the "I know him" or "I'll use my network" mentality. Entrepreneurs, in particular, are rather prone to this. In the process they ignore the job description, the candidate profile, the very definition of the job, the core competences and whether their crony can actually do the job. If the director thinks he knows the right person, that is fine, but that person will still need to go through the formal, agreed recruitment process.

BACK TO BASICS

It would be wise if more directors started with what they have got. The corporate world is full of businessmen who can see the grand plan, but fail to see that they have not the people to implement it. The best companies win when they make implementation the name of the game. They encourage their staff to deliver.

A director can have all the ideas possible but if he has not got the people to execute them he will assuredly fail. A strategy can be well thought out but poorly executed and disaster will follow. It can be part of the same thing. Some directors appear to be even more successful because, unlike their routine-thinking colleagues, they will not talk about the size of the deal but about its integration and complexity.

There is a propensity in life, and corporate life is no exception, when cornered and when egos are vulnerable, for directors to throw good money after bad. If a mistake has been made, exit and quickly with as much grace as possible, in order not to upset too many people or institutions. The City will appreciate it. The alternative will be to destroy even more. To be bold and cut the ties does not involve as much courage, in practice, as staying in.

Boldness becomes scarce when directors do not want to upset either their colleagues, or the City. But that is a wrong and costly attitude to adopt. Directors should be prepared to upset people, whether in the company or outside. They should have no truck with misplaced sentiment that prevents directors executing policies which they know are right when viewed from the longer perspective.

Oddly, perhaps, the successful ability to challenge is largely a reflection of the structure of the board itself. If divisional managing directors are on the board, there will be less real challenge. To criticise one's colleague merely leads to the others doing likewise about their patch. Hence the better boards are moving away from a composition based on divisions in favour of one based on functions. Then there will be challenge and tension between marketing and finance, and that is healthy.

But even then it can all go wrong. If the board is, in reality, two groupings – perhaps the CEO and the finance director in one group acting in unison, agreeing the outcome prior to the board meeting – the others will feel and be second-best, look superfluous and add little. It is difficult for one to challenge two. There are CEOs who will put an item on the agenda only when they know that they have a majority, and have stitched up the agenda and debate. It shows lack of confidence on the part of the CEO and reveals his ignorance of what a board is all about!

Boards go awry, too, when they do not know what the business of their board is and the special, peculiar style they need to adopt in their situation. In fact, different boards will consider different levels of detail which will determine whether the board has a natural propensity towards an executive committee format or not. If the industry is a "basic" one – for instance, construction – the board will be prone towards acting in the style of an executive committee. Their main activity is rather basic and the board will reflect this by deliberating on basic detail. (Also coupled with the style which is related to the industry is a propensity for certain boards to spend more time on particular items. The construction industry one, for example, will debate health and safety more thoroughly and frequently than, say, a retail board.) And beware, there is no point in having directors from a different culture joining such a board. They should come from an equally "focused" environment. Such boards operate as if they are virtually a division of a group.

Frequently, a director, rounded and experienced, will take decisions without realising how clever or original he is being. It is illustrated perhaps best in the case of the director who is also an

NED. He will have the opportunity to sit on another board and realise how much he knows – as well as to appreciate that the other person's grass is no greener. It is both a salutary and stimulating experience. Mind you, it can be easier to be an adviser and be effective, than to be the executive director who needs to do the implementing!

The UK has taken a unique and peculiar route in the last 30-plus years, regarding accountancy, and preferably chartered rather than certified, as the best generalist management education possible. Continental partners and the USA prefer the management schools. With 80 000 chartered accountants, the UK enjoys the dubious corporate advantage of having 20 times as many as its nearest continental rivals and more than the population of Antigua and Barbuda – man, woman and child. And remember – energy, flair and accountancy do not naturally go together. (It is also worth noting, in passing, two further aspects; a partnership, even the large modern ones, has a structure and psychology altogether different from that of a plc and therefore from the companies they audit. And while the auditors audit the companies, who audits the auditors? One or two of the big firms voluntarily audit each other, and the Audit Foundation is playing its part but the majority are not audited and none with the relish and gusto they show when auditing their clients and as unprofessionally as some now appear to be doing.)

MISPLACED SYMPATHY

Sometimes one can feel sorry for the director. Faced with so many issues, often concurrently; some predictable, others not; and often let down by professional advisers, with a thin line between success and failure – no wonder stress is all around. To add to his problems, demands change as the company changes. When expanding, for instance, companies usually run out of management. There are simply not the skill sets available.

What is happening here is the company lacks both foresight and planning. Foresight means developing existing staff (on the whole, growing companies blithely ignore such sophistication). If the skill sets are not available in their sector, then they should look at a related one for the basic ingredients. It can be done. If a company runs out of management and skills generally, it is because they have weak or non-existent personnel planning.

A director's fall can be quick and complete. Heroes, whether in the eyes of colleagues or the City, can tomorrow be pariahs; deliver a good performance one year and be labelled useless the next. Real success comes out of a mixture of competence, team effort, timing and luck – and you need luck especially – and any one of them can desert you.

Incidentally, a director is fortunate if he appoints more than about three good PAs in a career. A really good one will even be able to tell an enquirer how best to contact one of the company's NEDs. Most will not even know of his existence, adding that being non-executive, he does not have an office in the building. The enquirer knows that! But NEDs are legally part of the main team, and the fact that so many frontline staff of companies do not know who is on their board needs remedying.

Foolishly directors often pick at different layers, whichever looks to be the problem or whichever can give a quick fix – for the benefit of the City or his own reputation vis-à-vis his colleagues. Furthermore, depressingly, the majority of available talent can appear very commonplace. Mediocrity is alive and well. The overall standard of many in senior positions is actually rather ordinary. The outsider should never cease to be surprised at the apparently low standard of those purporting to be running the largest or most successful enterprises. Perhaps they are better in the different environment of their office, or in the boardroom, or when among colleagues and, therefore, on home ground, where they do not need to take into account what others have said before them or are likely to say afterwards. On the other hand, there is a growing cadre of excellence, the equal or the superior of many on the international scene, even if their formal training appears rather meagre in comparison.

The fact that many business people are poor public speakers does not help themselves or their companies – nor, indeed, the status and value society places on the wealth creators. The wealth created by effective directors can be so influential in the paying for and running of society as a whole, that it is easy for directors to believe that they are more important than others. Their wealth generation pays many of the bills for those who are, apparently, utterly divorced from business. Surprisingly, directors on the whole are rather shy or circumspect about their relevance apart from a group who are larger than life, or behave as if they are as successful as their egos tell them or their PR machine implies. But captains of industry are no more important than their academic counterparts, or than a director of a museum or a head teacher.

Indeed, the efforts of non-business people might be more permanent and therefore possibly more important. To ignite the spark of curiosity in a child, to make people aware of their past and of why we are different from other nations or how we reached the society we enjoy today, is fundamental by any definition of importance. Perhaps a director should be more tempted to stand up for the relevance of business. After all, in the few societies that are more prosperous and successful than the UK, such as the USA, the stature of the director is higher. The unwise director assumes that he is indispensable when he is not. Some are more key than others but all as individuals are expendable.

To their peers the pervading ordinariness of business leaders is partly explained by proximity and familiarity. Indeed, it is not a good thing to get too close – even if it were possible – to your idols, whatever walk of life they might be in. Even the person who dresses the king has no idols – he sees his monarch with nothing on, stripped of the trappings of office and the symbolism of power. Or possibly, ultimately, in the case of companies, the leader's ordinariness can be explained simply by stressing that business is not a difficult exercise, it is just made to look so.

THE COMPANY SECRETARY

When a director is newly appointed, whether executive or non-executive, one of his first acts should be to knock on the door of the company secretary. Oddly, many directors ignore the company secretary. Of course, in smaller companies he will probably be a main board director who combines two roles. In the case of larger companies, though, matters are very different. The roles are divorced and the company secretary is not, on the whole, on the main board. And yet he is the eyes and ears of that board, writing the minutes, knowing the history of the board's agenda – why certain items are on, which ones have been on in the past, and so on. Foolish is the director, and especially the NED, who does not befriend and consult the company secretary. In fact, the modern company secretary is at the centre of the corporate web. He can register the presence of the smallest fly impaled in the web and then advise the appropriate director accordingly. Indeed, contemporary company secretaries are becoming like general counsel in the USA, and that means becoming one of the half dozen key positions within the company. Why, therefore, ignore such a person, who, in the UK at least, is not in a position to be a direct threat; merely to offer a helping hand?

A TIME TO ARRIVE AND A TIME TO DEPART

There should be a baggage weight limit for directors. There is freedom of action for the director who has no baggage. He does not need to queue at the corporate reclaim desk. But how does a director travel lightly? The longer a director is in a company, the more baggage he accumulates. However, he needs to be bold in his thinking even if not necessarily in his action, during the initial period – a sort of corporate equivalent of the political 100 or 1000 days. Much subsequent performance originates from that period. Just as important as knowing how to present and package yourself to a prospective employer is the ability to know when to leave a company. To do it voluntarily, with your halo in place, and satisfaction all around, is an art in itself, whether as an executive or non-executive director. And there is a third element to the employment equation – what papers to leave behind that will not act to foster recriminations against you!

There is constant pressure on the good to move on, to believe that the other person's grass is greener and that they are being undervalued at their present company. Directors do not compare like with like, and usually leave a discussion feeling bruised and used, when probably, very possibly, the opposite is the case. Alas, a company can also lose good people when it is focussed, and this is a pity. After all, to be penalised for being effective and disciplined in business generally is, in one respect, hardly fair or encouraging.

There are no hard and fast rules on how long to stay, especially as an executive but also as a non-executive director. The style of the company; the director's own basic continued enthusiasm for the job or the general level of activity of the company – new acquisitions, disposals, etc.; new government regulations; the convenience of leaving the board; the message the director's departure might give – are among many other factors to bear in mind. (It is worth remembering, incidentally, that it can be peculiarly difficult to transfer from one culture to another – not just from or to a "basic" industry. This may be because such a move was largely involuntary – an apparent job for life, a career with one sector, as was once the case in retail banking and in the accountancy profession, but is no longer a probability; or where the move is from a decentralised group to a centralised one, or from a family-owned firm or where the family culture remains strong, into a well established plc.)

However, there is also another factor to consider. There are circumstances when the director is doing well, is much appreciated by all and is almost automatically associated with the company, but he concludes, rightly, that there is simply nowhere else to go within the firm. Moreover, the best will leave if the company is no longer able to offer real challenges. Nothing short of the right challenge will induce the more able to stay. The dilemma for directors is to maintain a reasonable set of challenges for those they want to keep without creating meaningless jobs.

With the departure of a senior, successful colleague a number of pressures build up. There is a loss of gravitas and social and technical skills. (The problem is equally prevalent at lower levels within the firm, where there is more interface with the public or the customer.) Senior directors retire early because they are tired or have made enough money or want to pursue a totally different career. They are the first generation who have been able to do so and the choice can be made as early as 50.

These directors often make one of two mistakes. First, they may have been inordinately busy hitherto as an executive director, with head down, judged on the executive side of the desk, and unable to assume a parallel, non-executive career. Or second, their firms may have discouraged such aspirations (in practice companies are becoming more open-minded in this crucial respect). So directors retire on the Friday and expect an NED career to start on the following Monday. But it will not. There are a lot of equally able people around. Also, their CVs do not make them appear different – if the candidate has gone via an outplacement firm the CV will look remarkably similar to a host of others: "a senior executive director of a major firm with a proven track record". Or they interview badly or they are unlucky. Maybe their careers are confined to one or two firms, making them much less attractive than those with a more eclectic background.

It is only second-best to be with one company for most of a corporate life and to argue that the company has changed beyond all recognition – due perhaps to deregulation, merger, back to core activities. It is still a variation on a theme.

If a director wishes to work for one company or somehow time has passed him by, then he should, as a minimum, supplement that experience with an NED position – and in a different sector.

There is almost a formula along the lines that for each company in which a director works, as long as his move is logical or subsequently vindicated, his worth to others increases by a factor of two and if to a different sector by a factor of three. If it is to a company where the stage of its development is radically different from his existing one, the increase in value is four times as great. Finally, if the experience is then further enhanced via an NED position the director will be unrecognisable from the relatively narrow-minded corporate version suggested above.

Even the most able directors have a problem with the selection process, both for themselves as candidates and as interviewers. It is often a question of the blind leading the blind, the interviewer not being used to interviewing and the interviewee not used to being interviewed. Gaps in the CV are not filled in, bland statements are not challenged, inaccuracies are left unchallenged and listed achievements, which might be largely bogus or exaggerated or should not be credited to one person, are allowed to take on the mantle of reality.

The main onus oddly is on the interviewee. He should ensure that all the relevant questions are asked. Usually the interviewer will be grateful, and the candidate content. Sometimes the candidate might think that he is being bumptious and brash. It might sound like that to him but not to the interviewer. Sometimes candidates assume that their achievements are sufficiently well known not to explain further. Usually this is not the case in practice, and another opportunity passes, for both of them. The least the candidate should do is to detail the facts and figures, comparisons with the start and finish of his period of office, even perhaps compared with the sector.

The same principle can extend back to his schooldays; if the team he was in was the best of its era, he should mention that. He should not assume that anybody but his proud parents can remember it.

SUCCESS AND FAILURE

And what about listing failures? Practically nobody ever does. It will be a wonderful day when a candidate says, "I went to jail between 1994 and 1995, but I have learnt a lot and if the same situation arose I would recognise it coming." Magic, pure magic. The failure might have been worse had he not been at the helm and it makes his successes seem that much more genuine. "Failures" are also useful and constructive to both the individual and the company, because a director sometimes needs a setback in order to learn. Why be so hesitant and apologetic about confessing weaknesses and relative failures when we all have the first and make the second? The more combat-proven the person, the more effective he will be; as mentioned previously, a great deal is learned by both the candidate and the interviewer from how the former reacts to adversity. Surely it is better to have such a colleague than his blinkered, blinded and bigoted counterpart?

Candidates complain that some headhunters want just two pages in a CV; others want as many as possible. The best rule is to give a summary, followed by detail, running into at least four more pages. The professionals will then have a quarry to dig into. The format is the preserve of the headhunters. You cannot win. Some want one way, others another. Let the headhunters rearrange according to their preferences.

Furthermore, a director will be serving his company well if he refrains from recruiting other than the very best possible candidates. Better by far not to recruit than to recruit second-best, and a director should not hesitate to attract the best. There is a fear among some of what a good person might do. Odd, but self-interest and self-defence eats away at the psyche of some directors.

It is better to explain to board colleagues that his senior team is to remain incomplete for an indefinite period and that taking no action other than continuing to search is a positive decision. As the candidate, however, it is not necessarily ideal to succeed a success-ful person! The chances are that the new director will come a cropper. The conundrum, from a cynical perspective, is that a successful director will want to appoint a less able successor. In that way, his own achievements will glitter even more.

And if the director earns a high remuneration package for trying and succeeding, his colleagues and the shareholders should not begrudge him his worth. Employees take no risks; directors do, and the latter have temptation placed in their human path.

With longevity can come integrity; those with integrity will last a long time in most conventional plcs and even in a family firm. And long-term relationships with clients are achieved only on the back of integrity. Also to be borne in mind, though, is the dilemma which can arise if a director is *in situ* too long; he will have to keep justifying his past decisions. Interestingly, this is a very good reason why a CEO should not become chairman of the same company. He developed the strategy and will, even as chairman, be protective of it, for that strategy will be based on his past decisions.

There are some boards which have benefited incalculably from being together for a long time, for perhaps as long as eight to ten years. There is a need for the external recruit now and again, but the long-established team will not be diluted or be broken in the process. It is sad, therefore, as a long-established team can be so effective, that the City attaches little value to it. It is not what those institutions concentrate on.

Alas, long-term relationships with financial advisers, based on the integrity of the individuals, is becoming a rarity despite its mutual value (see Chapter 3). The benefit never survives the departure of one or other in the relationship. The likelihood of re-establishing a similar relationship has been greatly reduced as a direct consequent of the Americanisation of the City where the philosophy is blunt and very clear – go out and get business! Perhaps in the end, the new modern approach of transitory associations with little personal chemistry is a way of avoiding a long-term relationship descending into complacency!

Finally, there are companies which do not appreciate the real value of a director until or unless he leaves. It is rather like good health, only fully appreciated when what was taken for granted has been taken away.

Just as the best publicists are paid to keep their clients out of the press as well as in (on their terms), so the best directors should be rewarded for avoiding mistakes rather than only for their successes. Alas, the City gives them little credit and in fairness may not, in most instances, even know that a director has deftly avoided a costly mistake. No goodwill accumulates to capitalise on when, or possibly if, the going gets tough. To do nothing, or to prevent something happening or, on occasion, to say "No" and for it to be regarded as a positive contribution are among the best contributions a director can make at board level.

A director will be acting positively if he resists the temptation of making an acquisition in haste. What might appear a "good thing" can turn out to be a misguided corporate ego trip, implemented under pressure or in near-panic conditions and the consequences usually will be dire. A big takeover, even if successfully executed at the time and generally deemed to make some conventional sense, is nonetheless opening the door to a hostile world for the success-ful director. Unless he plans to be around for the next five years he might as well not be part of the future. He will have engineered, unplanned, his premature departure.

MITIGATING FAILURE

If a director fails, for whatever reason – as long as it is not because of dishonesty, overt arrogance or total transparent incompetence – there are ways of clawing back up the corporate ladder.

A word of caution. To reach the top originally, the director will inevitably have had to beat many people. Years later these apparently long-forgotten skirmishes among those who appear to have become trusted friends or, at least, business colleagues, can actually hold back the director's career. A sore can fester longer than the successful director realises and, as touched on before, when the latter asks the former for a reference – possibly when seeking an NED position – the hint of not being good enough can be conveyed damagingly. Doors close with the gentlest of clicks.

Directors can have a reputation for good or bad which is often largely unwarranted but nevertheless can attach permanently to the person concerned. There is not necessarily much logic to that indictment; it can be grossly unfair. Nor is it just a question of the City being at the losing end of a deal in which the director was the victor. In fact, often, such directors gain extra credit from the losing financial service company; if they cannot beat them they might at least admire them.

Then there are the lucky ones who do not need to bounce back because they are never down. They are lucky for they are usually no better than the ones who either just fail – and the line between success or failure can, as observed, be a narrow one – or bear no comparison with the ones who take up the bigger challenge.

Some directors are inordinately lucky. A director can make a profit, to all intents and purposes, by "merely" stripping out, leaving nothing of value for the longer term, but giving the impression of a lean, successful, focussed organisation, whereas in reality there is probably nothing left. The shareholders lose out, the share price goes down and then – the ultimate ignominy – the company is taken over. NEDs will need to understand and prevent that happening. A company needs to survive beyond the current climate, not survive in order to die. What the director has also managed to do is stifle intellectual curiosity. Even where a major overhaul needs to happen, the director must also possess the skill of building again, of healing. If all he knows is how to break a group up, he is not the right person for the next stage.

Sometimes a director under pressure or out to impress will put in excessively long hours. It should not be a question of the longevity of effort but rather its degree of relevance. The best directors lead a balanced existence which also means time to be with their families, especially their children, to have outside interests and to take regular holidays. Variety gives spice and freshness to a director's deliberations. Taking work home merely prevents the director recuperating; it makes him stale.

Or a director under pressure might resort to cutting back on development programmes, which can be a short cut to profitability but it is a shorter cut still to long-term survival and greater profits. It may be necessary to cut off development programmes and it might take great courage to do so. The director will need to show little emotion and much incisiveness. It is easy to err on either side of the dividing line.

Some directors attempt to disguise their shortcomings by setting a conservative budget, one that is easy to meet, and fooling themselves and some colleagues that all is well. But is that really creating shareholder value or keeping an eye on the longer term? It is probably better to set a realistically ambitious one and fall slightly short.

Corporate life is blessed with an able group – not large, and not the majority but an effective and valuable minority – who will attempt to win where others have failed. They are the builders of a business from whatever foundation or inheritance they were given. If they subsequently fail, failure might have been greater had they not been at the helm, and they deserve credit. However, there is no excuse or justification to hero-worship them. Most of them know how to play the corporate PR game and they do it subtly and almost imperceptibly. To acquire a company or to turn one around, or merely to direct a company at a time of great potential change and challenge, requires from the director the ability to appear initially pessimistic and then pleasantly surprised!

Sometimes a firm unintentionally almost encourages a director to make a mistake by imposing a financial ceiling on each director – rightly – but putting no equivalent limit on a contract he might negotiate. A contract that goes wrong can be more expensive and put the company to greater financial risk and exposure.

Some directors have a facility to bounce back, to the marvel of their adherents and to the consternation of others. Some do their escape acts too quickly before the end of the conventionally recognised period of corporate mourning.

One route back, alas and strangely, is to join a group of companies which, surprisingly, do not seek to recruit the best. They are happy not to disrupt the gentle flow of business life, which generally has been upwards or satisfactory and where the company believes it has a special niche in its marketplace or understanding of how the sector works. On the whole, however, getting back up the corporate ladder is as hard, if not harder, than the original journey.

8
STRUCTURES AND STRATEGIES

Just as it was fashionable for politicians at the end of the 20th century to talk of "the economy, stupid", when asked what was the most important aspect of their job, the successful business person could substitute "strategy" for "economy". Even so, it is important not to isolate strategy but to couple it inextricably with the word "structure". Every company needs to put up its flag in order to say that it stands for something and that it has reached a certain stage, whether that is merely base camp or it is about to ascend the peak. Before that, however, it will need to ensure that its strategy and structure are the correct ones.

However, we need to be clear why companies need strategies, how they should be formulated, implemented and updated – the process of reviewing – and finally how the processes and structures can reflect this dynamic, ongoing exercise.

WHY A STRATEGY

Companies often fall into a number of different traps. They may create a strategy only from the top downwards instead of allowing elements of it to percolate up from the various divisions (without, heaven forbid, neglecting their ultimate responsibility). They may regard the strategy as sacrosanct and inflexible and so not to be tampered with or tailored to changing circumstances; or they may produce a strategy which is, in practice, unrealistic for the company concerned – the organisation might not have either the reputation, the people or the position in their sector to execute it effectively.

There is an evolutionary process in companies and the strategy, in its various manifestations, will or should reflect these phases. The stages are simple. Initially, the entrepreneur deliberates in detail on all aspects and when, because of growth, he cannot know everything in such detail, relevant strategies and structures evolve. All companies surely want to grow; if they did not their share-holders would ask why and probably want their money back. But to grow requires a strong, clear, relevant strategy and evidence of the ability to execute it.

In business, it can be much easier to succeed via a failed company than to set out initially with nothing other than a business plan and high hopes. At least, in the case of the former, the company will have experience, the staff *in situ* and the management had possibly "only" got their strategy wrong. With the right strategy it could come together more quickly than if they set out with nothing. It becomes a matter, above all, of trying to determine next time around how the market will move.

Starting a business is very difficult. Start-ups take longer to establish than planned and they also tend to absorb more money than assumed. At least an existing company, however poor its state of health, will have more momentum and be the cheaper – though not necessarily cheap – route forward. It is also easy to improve on other people and hard to improve on oneself! Starting afresh – unless there is a brilliant idea – and creating the effective strategy to accompany it, is a painful process.

And remember that it is remarkably easy to get into new activities but it is often extraordinarily difficult to get out of them. So developing the strategy is a very serious exercise.

Once the strategy has been decided and the psychological framework established, practically all executive decisions will be taken under the auspices of the simple question, "Does it fit the strategy?" A strategy can be well thought out but poorly executed and that leads to disaster. Even the evolution of the strategy can take a long time and can often be a painful exercise. It is essential that a company never delays unduly the implementation of its strategy, once it has been agreed.

Invariably, when a company issues a profits warning, analysts will focus on the company's strategy. It is not, therefore, an idle exercise or an ego trip but rather a fundamental tool and corner-stone of corporate survival. However, strategies *can* become ego trips or be too grand and consequently make cash flow even more strained and crucial. This is where one of the less developed and more secretive roles of a non-executive director plays a fuller part; they, divorced from the daily running of the company, should be there to prick the egos of these grand designs.

NEDs are not there to spoil an appropriate deal but to ensure that all the facts are discussed thoroughly in a proper, conventional, commercial way; having less data they can also see the general picture which their executive colleagues may not, being either functional heads or responsible for stand-alone divisions. (Indeed, many directors suffer from allowing themselves to be governed by data. Data can create two obstacles to effective management; it is by definition always history and the director who relies heavily on data will almost certainly act as if he is on the executive committee, not on the main board.)

THE DYNAMICS OF STRATEGIES

Only a corporate blockhead would regard strategy as merely a once-a-year exercise rather than a gradual one. Strategy is a truly dynamic entity and the route to the endgame has many paths. Sometimes it might not be a matter of proceeding via the most direct route. Alas, despite its pivotal importance, strategy as a topic lacks one crucial characteristic – it does not instantly affect the bottom line unless the company is in desperate straits and is being run by a company doctor. So the CEO under pressure, or inexperienced, or operating within a corporate culture, undisciplined or unfamiliar with the strictness of evolving strategies, is a high-risk patient. (In practice, many companies fudge their strategic reviews. They do not even see the real need for major strategic change and so tinker with it. They fool nobody but themselves. Generally, the very strategically aware companies tend to be the larger ones. They become strategy-orientated to a peculiar and fascinating degree, endlessly assessing, interpreting and refining, in the context of looking at how the industry outside is developing.)

Inevitably, there will be moments during the implementation of a strategy when the company will go through tough times. It is important, therefore, that all relevant managers and directors are supportive of it. The only way that this can be assured is to secure a shared authorship and ownership of the strategy. Indeed, it is not the role of a main board nor do they have the time to be the sole author of the group strategy. They are there to set the crucial parameters; then co-ordinate, finalise and execute.

FEET ON THE GROUND

When evolving a strategy, a company should start with what it has got. A naive and obvious statement? The corporate world is strewn with sad cases of boards of directors who can see the grand designs but who do not devote sufficient time and effort to analysing whether they have the appropriate people, technical skills or even reputation. But even if all the ducks are in a row, a company will need the best possible operational managers in order to deliver the strategy – to make it happen. And "best" can mean having colleagues who will put in the detailed work.

There is a textbook philosophy, underlined by the business schools and generally a very sound yardstick to aim for: aim to be a major player within three years, otherwise do not be in that area at all. Equally, it is normally best to dispose of a division or subsidiary if your presence is a merely fragmented one.

A director would be wise to ask where the real value is in his organisation. What are the core values? Cunningly, the best boards also ensure that they see how the strategy is executed. They go to where it is happening, otherwise there is no possibility of assessing it correctly. Boards need to know how colleagues tick. If the board becomes isolated from the execution of strategy, it will not see the problems early enough.

Sometimes, it is necessary to downsize in order to grow. In the good times, directors can get bored with the basics; it becomes uninspiring even if profitable. Certainly in times of recession it is a question of back to core activities even though such an exercise can be emotionally draining and difficult for existing executives to implement; some of them will have been responsible for acquiring the companies that constitute the non-core activities. It can be further compounded if a non-core part is performing better than the core. The only way forward is to ensure that the non-executive team, and in particular the chairman – who should have no attachment or sentiment – convince their executive colleagues that, being non-core, they can be sold and at a high price because they are doing well. The monies can then be reinvested in a core activity.

Cutting across all debate on strategy is the relentless increase in overheads. It appears to be both inevitable and unremitting. While overheads rise, the discussions that accompany the subject are usually draining. It can be better to cut by an arbitrary figure – perhaps by 1 per cent – and just do it. Be more interested in taking action than in the detail.

Many companies merely tread water; turnover increases, margins might get better, but somehow profit remains either static or reduces. The reason is because overheads are allowed to increase. The problem with overheads is that colleagues argue that an increase in expenditure is necessary before a saving or an increase in profits will be achieved. Unfortunately, the latter often fails to materialise whereas the former certainly will. Remember, also, that overheads tend to rise quicker where the interests of a group of colleagues is greatest! And *even if* the profit margins *are* achieved, there is associated pain.

AN ELEMENT OFTEN IGNORED

Growth, like profit, is a mixed blessing. Growth can actually spoil a company if the strategy does not reflect the reality. If a company finds itself faced with demands for growth yet it has not the resources to accommodate it, the only solution may be to sell and start again. (And remember, as in the animal kingdom so in the business world, what is the demise of one is an opportunity for another. There is nothing sacrosanct, no divine right to be the king of any jungle.)

The two basic types of growth are growth that increases the value of the company and growth that increases profit. A company can go on a Mickey Mouse spree, create "Mickey Mouse International", but people will ask, "But what are they doing?" "What does the company stand for?" Such growth confuses people – employees, advisers, customers, the business press, everybody. It is a primary role of the NEDs to say to the executive directors, "Stop it!"

Most companies are a balance between rigour and vigour, or slow progress versus growth. Managing both within the same group requires great and different skills. Big growth usually means not just growth, but heavy investment and commitment, and that can just as easily equal losses. Boards and, if possible, shareholders need to ask whether there is rigour underlining the vigour!

While growth can be a mixed blessing, mere survival is insufficient. Unfortunately, successful companies are prone to complacency and are subject to comparing themselves with internally set yardsticks, forgetting, in the meantime, that the competition is not standing still. The company may panic and decide to appear to be doing something positive, such as enhancing shareholder value and making an acquisition. It is a hazardous occupation at the best of times to acquire a company with its different culture, people, expectations, and at the cost, both upfront and hidden. To contemplate an acquisition in these contrived and undisciplined circumstances is tempting calamity.

Conservative-minded companies, proud of their identity and past records, are often the ones least well equipped to face the future. They do not learn enough from the fast-growing ones – from the recently established competition, which they probably either ignore or treat with contempt, justifying their stance on the likelihood that the new company will be merely a shooting star. Amazingly, these same companies are probably, by definition, quite long established. They may be conservative but the older the company the more transitions they will have been through. Why can they not capitalise on their ability to survive rather than allow their mere longevity to become a dangerous element in their final demise? It is no good having an historically right business. It needs to represent what is right today.

A note of caution. If your company is a clear market leader do not wrap yourself in euphoria. It may be due largely to the fact that the potential competition could not be bothered to enter the marketplace or devote sufficient resources to overtake the market leader. And the reason for that could be quite simply that the opportunities do not actually warrant the necessary resources. (A vacancy may arise in this rarefied niche market with the demise of one of the few companies operating in that sector. Interestingly, the failure of the company which others might hope to replace will almost certainly be due to its own arrogance, believing that it is in an unassailable position and therefore need not listen to its customers but merely give lip service to client needs; yet, meanwhile, carrying on doing its own thing).

STRATEGIC ACQUISITIONS

An acquisition can look sexy at the time but organic growth is usually the safer option. It can be both exacting and awkward to merge two separate, corporate cultures and then expect the chemistry to cement the new group. (In practice, regardless of the intention or declared goals, one never gets a merger of equals; a dominant partner emerges.) Furthermore, most of the directors involved tend to overestimate the drivers and underestimate the cultural difficulties. As in the song, they are more like cockeyed optimists. However, these portents make not one iota of difference; the human urge to acquire appears unstoppable. And you do not change a company culture, or satisfy the new structural requirements, merely by changing the group logo. In fact, some companies, rightly, develop the approach of a strong decentralised and devolved authority and put in place the crucial financial controls. All very fine. Those controls will, hopefully, be based on cash, and each subsidiary will be incentivised, and will attempt to attract the best people, train them and give them the controlled freedom to get on with it. Bluntly, all companies need to have in place the appropriate degree of controls from day one. They will need to know what is actually going on and that means, as a first step, obtaining the relevant, basic data – and on time. (Acquisitions are never what they appear. It is worse even than that! If the takeover is not hostile it could be a matter of the other directors wanting to sell because they have a reason to do so. The former must exhaustively analyse the reasons to ensure that what appears to be on offer is the reality.)

There is a special challenge for the finance director when an acquisition has been made – or when the group needs to refocus.

The temptation is to analyse and tackle things sector by sector, division by division. The right approach, however, is to conduct the exercise more speedily and across the company; otherwise industrial business cycles, or even the programme of board meetings, could force the company to decide – or worse still, buy or sell – in a dip.

AN EXTERNAL CHALLENGE TO THE STRATEGY

The rules have changed for all participants in a takeover, merger or acquisition. Until recently, a CEO could politely or impolitely tell an unwelcome bidder to go elsewhere, and his advisers would probably back him. Now, the role of the Financial Services Authority and the obligations on all to check everything – written and verbal – before doing or saying anything with a verification note before any utterances has meant that the takeover, etc. is now run mainly by lawyers, accountants and investment bankers, rather than by boards. Nowadays, a CEO can only tell a hostile bidder to go away if his advisers agree with him. As a result, something has been lost in the process.

Boards would do well to remember that a hostile bid is won or lost in the first 24 hours. Tragically, yet understandably, boards are usually unprepared either for hostile or for friendly bids. If the directors manage, via luck or judgement, to buy themselves a delay of three or four days after the shock wave first hits their boardroom door, they will be able to react sensibly as part of a likely successful defence. If the board and company survive, they have a golden opportunity to learn about their own company and to come through the saga a better organisation. Oddly, perhaps, an unsuccessful hostile bid can prove a constructive and beneficial exercise for the receiving board! Some organisations need a crisis in order to make overdue decisions.

Sometimes the necessary changes are not difficult to achieve; it is making them permanent that is difficult. There is a need to make the minimum number of board changes as possible, or at least in a short period of time. There can be too much change too quickly for the health of an organisation.

Companies fail to establish effective control systems. Companies need to rely heavily on their own management accounts in order to keep things under tight control; otherwise, there will be a large black hole. But there is a price to pay; first-rate internal mechanisms of checks and balances may require a director to stand up to a colleague and report him to his superior, even bringing the matter to the main board. This takes considerable courage and it can be a personal gamble.

(Generally, avoid having a board meeting too close to the publishing of the management accounts; it changes the style of the meeting.) External audits cover only about 60 per cent of the total picture. But, as recent events have shown, even the 60 per cent might be inadequately covered. The external audit is not going to save reputations or even companies and auditors issue pages of disclaimers in an attempt to protect themselves.

STRATEGY AND SUCCESSION PLANNING

The overall value of a company is often largely dependent upon the quality of the planned succession. (It is not only potential successors who have more than a passing interest here, nor even the company as a whole or the shareholders and the City. As mentioned in Chapter 5, the customer may also be worried – yet few

boards consider their anxieties, until they affect the bottom line.)
An acquisition, takeover or some other non-organic activity can
throw the whole equation off balance and create far more
dissatisfaction than some will realise until it is too late. For every
one individual who perceives the exercise as a God-sent opportunity, there will be many who will think the opposite. Nor might
there be much time to satisfy the cadre of bruised or dented egos. It
can take at least six months for a board to settle in.

Furthermore, if a senior director was previously a big fish in a
small pond, and is now the opposite following the merger, there
will be a cultural misfit and no structure will be adequate in his
mind to redress this imbalance and threat. Not surprisingly,
therefore, it is often better to concentrate on organic growth –
usually unspectacular, of little commercial profit to the City but a
great deal safer, and more logical in the majority of cases. (Of
course, the City might not allow this route, especially if the
company is a mature one, needing further growth in the City's eyes
and for their purposes, but not necessarily the purposes of the
client.) Concentration on organic growth also enables the company
structure and strategy to correspond more precisely and so serve
the overall corporate goals more effectively. In short, with organic
growth the company can control the situation.

Also, there is a need to do a thorough audit on the other company's corporate culture to see what relationship the senior and
other personnel have with that culture. In some instances, the
culture is subservient to the top personnel; in others, the reverse.
To get it wrong is like putting a square peg in a round hole, with a
large price tag attached. In some firms, those working there are
subservient to the corporate cultures; in others the opposite is the
case. Where employees are not subservient, change is usually

easier to bring about. Woe betide the company, however, that acquires another where the position of the people vis-à-vis the corporate culture is the opposite to their own.

Foolishly, many companies on the acquisition path fall flat on their corporate faces at the first meeting following the successful conclusion of the deal. The existing team will know more, much more, than the acquirer about their product, and in all technical ways. What the acquirer will or should offer, and therefore add constructively to the overall equation, is in areas such as better management, procedures and more effective marketing.

Directors can get locked into a mindset and, while it is exhausting and counterproductive to derail corporate thinking on a regular basis, there is a time for a radical rethink on strategy. One way is for the recently appointed chairman, even if he is promoted from within and was part-author of the existing strategy, to ask the CEO to go away and revisit the strategy – nothing to be off limits.

The initial reaction will be one of shock; but if the CEO is given a finite timetable – perhaps no more than four months – he will possibly return with a major revamp. Then the suspense begins. The board will be tested. How will they respond? If, after due debate, they reject the proposals, that equals a vote of no confidence in the CEO! So it will be a gamble, but it may be one worth taking, and it will not be so radical a gamble in practice. The board will have been consulted at every stage of the strategic review.

Businesses in acquisitive mode would do well to remember – or even to know – that it can be difficult to absorb small acquisitions and mould them into a larger, logical one. It is difficult enough trying to incorporate small bits of companies already in the group into a meaningful whole.

Also, a board should never be too trusting, especially in the case of a takeover. Even if your side has followed every step and clause of the Takeover Panel Code, others will not necessarily have done so even if, at a glance, it appears that they have.

On a more mundane and routine level, if a company should be decentralised but is not, that constitutes a fundamental problem, and vice versa the same applies. In fact, what is the modern corporate head office for? Is it merely a place, a global concept? If an enthusiastic chief executive decides to find out, the initial enthusiasm will quickly evaporate to be replaced by resistance from suspicious senior colleagues.

UNSEXY, BUT SOUND

Inevitably, for some companies at certain times and in certain circumstances, non-organic growth is the right executive decision. To miss that chance is to fail the company and its interested parties. Such is the conundrum of executive life! It is just that more are in favour of quick, high-profile solutions, where success fades quickly but not before a rather ineffectual remuneration committee has more than compensated and rewarded inadequate performance. Again, the company needs to ask, "What is our strategy?" The strategy should guide all investment decisions. Is the investment going to help deliver the strategy? At any time in a company's existence and evolution, strategy should be the centrally defining element, and all must know what business they are in. There will be no need to direct everybody all the time; they will be part of the strategy, of the process. The board will have laid the framework months before. Local managers will manage with a degree of independence and confidence – with the checks and balances and controls ultimately from the board. Time is often wasted because people come back to check because they do not know what the company is about. Beware, though; a successfully run company can mean that the very success is the precursor to carelessness and to the weakening of controls.

The acquirer is also there to back a good inherited team, to ascertain quickly which of their new staff are worth cultivating and to know when to put an arm round the right person when they are in trouble. Equally, if the team is poor, it is up to the new management to get rid of it. There is an old adage; it is a privilege to hire and a duty to fire. The CEO or other directors of the combined teams will learn one lesson very quickly if they did not know it already – leadership is lonely (especially if you are in the minority! Incidentally, if in a minority of one then there is something very wrong!).

Strategies and the accompanying structures can fail for other reasons. If an organisation is growing like Topsy, it means that the infrastructure is not in place; organisations are intrinsically unstable, whereas people are intrinsically stable.

BUDGETS AND STRATEGIES

To gauge the true performance of a company, beyond the routine management accounts, it is necessary to remain loyal to a set budget. (In fact, balance sheets tell almost nothing. A company can have a good, strong one and be broke! Able directors in well-run companies get the early warning signals from cash flow.) The perceptive analyst and NED understands and questions cash and rightly so. But cash flow is to be treated with care. The company accounts can show significant projects but they may not be cash profits – they may show releasing provisions, merger accounting (that is why a merger or acquisition can often look good and suddenly collapse).

Budgets are a better indicator as to whether a strategy is working than is often realised. Even a budget that appears to be failing should not be abandoned hastily. There may be inconsistencies but the budget does ensure discipline. Otherwise the firm does not know where it is going. There is no comparing of like with like, between two years.

The worst scenario is to re-budget and then monitor progress against that yardstick. By so doing the board forgets where reality is. The budget is the sum of a set of parts. If x happens then y will follow. A board might get something wrong but leave the original budget *in situ*. Overshooting a budget is as bad as undershooting!

There are two approaches to a budget. Some want to change it almost before the financial year has started while others argue that if the budget is wrong try to get back to it regardless. What is necessary here is to recognise being off target and attempt to get back on, rather than merely refocussing forecasts. If the budget is only slightly adrift then the finance director will, in addition to the budget, need to give the board quarterly forecasts. They will not constitute a change of budget, merely be forecasts. If, however, there is no chance of ever getting back on budget then, but only then, should the board contemplate changing the budget.

COMPANY POLITICS

Settling unhelpfully over all these combinations is the invidious influence of company politics. It can put a stop on the career of the ablest and give a helping hand to mediocrity. Some play the game, others cannot be bothered and others still do not know how to play. The eventual losers are the individuals, the company and even the strategy. There is a way of helping to eradicate this, or at least creating an environment where it is not likely to flourish. The more layers of management, the greater propensity there is for company politics. Therefore, keep the group structure simple and focussed. (Taking a tier out of the process means taking a tier out of management and that can prove very successful in cost-saving terms. Also, authority is finite. To create tiers means distributing a finite resource; it does not create additional authority. Remember, too, that the best run companies keep their structures simple.)

Also, be mindful that structures should not create a hiding place for the marginally competent person who will gain more credit than he deserves. If you allow an apparently successful colleague to move around the organisation, he may never be in one place long enough for his colleagues to really determine and measure how effective he was in his previous positions.

A FLATTER STRUCTURE

It is worth bearing in mind that, as a company's organisation becomes flatter, there will be fewer and fewer career opportunities which, in turn, will result in the more able people leaving. Some companies find it difficult enough to attract and develop the best but more find it harder to retain them. Often this can be a consequence of the tendency to have a flatter structure. If that is not enough of a nightmare, the prospect of being number two in the organisation is neither very satisfying nor stimulating. Equally, those who are second-in-command are often not very successful. They might be able but will possibly have little to do.

Despite the downside of having a flatter organisation, it is better, on the whole, to have as small a main board as possible. If the company gets into trouble, it will be grateful for that structural efficiency – making it easier to come to a consensus and then to execute the decisions. The smaller board also helps a company avoid getting into trouble in the first place. (It is little wonder that few businessmen want to join public government boards, despite their desire to contribute to the common good. With their large, cumbersome, representative compositions, the public bodies purport to be more business-orientated, remain unattractive and in a different league. A pity, because it means turning away real talent desperately needed in public life. Another problem for business people making the transition to a public appointment is that the selection process in order to appear transparent takes a long time. Moreover, it can take at least four times as long to make a decision in the public sector compared with the private.)

If the company is large, or is a conglomerate or is broken up into smaller divisions, the structure will need to be especially well managed. Otherwise, it can mean that the main board deliberations are dominated by talk and feedback from various smaller divisions. It discards the mantle of the main board for the pedantic detail of the executive committee, reflecting on a local basis. At best, a main board is reminiscent of a production line – with important but tedious and constant flows of management accounts, etc. Hence the need for directors, especially NEDs, to go for the factory or office tour, to visit the divisions, in order to see what is actually happening and then to build relationships with subsidiaries. (If decentralised, aim where possible to have a controlled decentralisation. It is quite impossible to run a decentralised group effectively from one point – anywhere on the globe.) The structure in place can act as a warning to directors. A complicated structure can mean trouble; it is harder to manage, and ripe for the greed and the covering up of corporate incompetence.

In the process of loosening ties between people and larger organisations, as the latter become less fashionable, there is a significant group of able people who will be left behind in the corporate ebbing and flowing of events. Those who work for the great and long-established concerns, such as BP and Ford, can claim many advantages – discipline of management accounts, succession planning, managing change, etc. – but if they ever choose to leave they will be especially difficult to place. Those people have become, for want of a better phrase, brainwashed. They will think, believe and rely on their deeply established corporate beliefs. Once an employee of such a firm, almost certainly, always so.

SPOTTING TRENDS, PREDICTING THE FUTURE

It is uncanny how sharp are the customer's antennae and how early they come into play – and how blunt and slow is the company's interpretation of the same information. Those closest to the company see trends least quickly and those at the top, generally, are the slowest of all to register. That result can be chaotic, even catastrophic. The later the reading of signs by the company, the more it will need to invest in both time and money to put it right – if it is even given the chance.

And what about the company that tries to predict ten years ahead and evolve an outline strategy to accompany it? Is it in cloud-cuckoo-land or will it be on cloud nine? Interestingly, some of the very best companies – those, as argued previously, that set the pace rather than react to events – tend to have pondered the furthest corporate horizons. Even a ten-year vision can be broken down into a mere 40 quarters! (As a rule of thumb, a director should give himself five minutes a day to look at the next five years. It can be in his bath, when shaving, when walking, when pushing the trolley around the supermarket.) An admirable annual exercise is to ask: What do we want the business to be in five years' time? If the suggested answer is to double turnover and maintain margins, how is this to be done? Will it sort of happen, or can it be managed and not rely heavily on luck? Whatever the manifestations are, whichever question is asked, it is now possible to send key staff on very good training courses, rather than rely on trial and error, and to thereby understand more fully how a team can evolve and together achieve results that are not unique and often, therefore, very achievable.

Remember, also, that certain industries are especially good early indicators of corporate trends. The clear bell-weather forecasters are advertising, retail banking, home building, high technology, consultancy, traditional manufacturing, general retail and even airlines. There is no excuse, therefore, for not reading, under-standing and seeing the signs.

(On occasion, in the process of pursuing a modern, efficient yet perhaps clinical, approach to corporate structures, characteristics of real value are lost. In the 19th century, mutuals were created to meet a business need and based on a social structure – the human urge to belong and be catered for. The mutual is now discarded by all but an isolated few. Yet the human and psychological basis for them remains true today. The company or sector that is able to evolve a modern equivalent will gain a strong commercial advantage.)

Moreover, in respect of people, a company can lose its best simply because opportunities tend to exist in organisations that are expanding. It is tough for the director who finds himself in the wrong organisation at the wrong time in the company's or the sector's business cycle or history. (Incidentally, if a company has reached its nadir and is in dire straits, the strategy will be simple: focus on the financial background.)

WORRYING TRENDS

It is somewhat disconcerting that a time when fashionable corporate talk is of teams in industry corresponds with a unique time in business, when there are more and new forces working in the opposite direction. Teleworking, increased flexibility, the general influence of IT and the greater movement of people between companies or establishing their own businesses are all working against teams. No one would advocate adopting Luddite tendencies, but an acknowledgement of the trends is a consideration at least. Moreover, the explosive manner in which IT has permeated the business world has meant to some – and to too many – that it can be a panacea. It enables directors to fudge certain decisions with untold yet dire consequences.

There is a philosophy, often adopted unconsciously, that states that a company with a problem merely needs to throw money at it, developing the "right" technology. In fact what is needed is to know where to go from here, how to achieve the goals and get the timing right, in order to shift the business model. In short: basic, routine, long-established, good business practice, which the director's grandfather would have been familiar with. The IT solution is a distraction or a temptation to adopt the wrong policies. It can be a black hole – directors feel they need to spend on it, because others do, and purchase the best and most sophisticated, because that must make commercial sense. It is quite calamitous.

Even if the company adopts the correct, balanced IT policy, it will probably still make somewhat of a hash of it all. IT systems are dynamic; they do not, therefore, stand still. There is no room to believe that the system is finally in place and the topic can now come off the agenda. It will need to be massaged and reviewed. No director should divorce technology from the business; there is a need to manage technology as a conventional management tool; not as a catalyst, which is somehow allowed to remain separate.

THE BOARD IN CRISIS: THE SPLIT

It is the boards of larger companies that have a greater tendency to split, rather than the mid cap organisations. If the company is a FTSE 100 or even up to 250 company, it may well have a chairman who is larger than life, and a CEO who is not far behind, with a finance director who wants to be, and another director sharing the same dream and aspiration! The NEDs will possibly be more used to getting their way than is healthy. The respectable-suited board is really a group of corporate arsonists!

The more "personalities" a board possesses, the more prone will be the board to splits. When there is a story about a boardroom split, it is nearly always about one of the big companies, and this is not only because bigger companies are more newsworthy.

THE BOARD AND AGMS/EGMS

Fortunately, most general meetings pass seamlessly into oblivion. The odds are stacked so heavily in favour of the board against all but the largest shareholder or most persistent OAP. The directors, collectively, need to be polite and controlled, to sit higher than the audience, to have microphones (and the shareholders not), to be patient and, above all, well briefed. There is a large minority of top businessmen who regret a single phrase and will never have the chance to live it down.

To be successful, therefore, a company needs to keep its structure simple, for the structure to reflect the strategy along with both the people's and the company's reputations. The strategy must have the right authorship, be flexibly interpreted yet remain in place in a recognised format. Turnover and/or profit are measures of the health and vibrancy of a company but they are not the main ones. Recruit the team, get it focussed, establish pride and leadership plus all the basic economic controls, and you have a good chance of making progress.

9
PSYCHOLOGY AND EMOTIONS

Some directors can believe their own publicity. The best are confident, energetic and tenacious; the worst believe in themselves to an unreasonable degree and are blind to realities. Some cannot even recognise a mistake when they make one. A more open, truthful attitude will benefit a director in a number of ways. Some would serve themselves and their organisations well if they relied a little more on their instincts. When a director fails it is surprisingly more often than realised due to him sounding the advice of others, rather than following his gut reactions. The "gut", or intuition, is more sophisticated and analytically active than is recognised.

THROUGH THE CORPORATE MAZE

It will prevent him from claiming something which another colleague might also claim and with more justification. Such farcical merry-go-rounds are not uncommon; it is merely somewhat rare for either to be aware of the antics of the other. But the merry-go-round does sometimes complete its circle and the claimants will be discredited in a way which is hard subsequently to explain; mere confusion and misunderstanding will not get the director off the hook.

After a time he believes that the figment of his imagination is indeed the reality. Often there is an element of justification for his claims. Few major initiatives or events have a single author. But the downside can raise its grim head in different ways, at different times and after many years. At interview, the interviewer, almost certainly more experienced in his role than is the interviewee in his, will note the discrepancies without revealing his conclusions. The candidate might offer as a referee former colleagues who will use that opportunity to settle an old score.

There are good mistakes and bad ones, and the making of the former is dependent upon the circumstances in which the mistake was made. Ideally, a director should encourage his younger protégé to make a mistake and learn from it. The younger the better, and better still if the age gap between the director and the protégé is as wide as possible. It is a benefit also if the "good mistake" was made at a location geographically some distance away from the director's corporate headquarters. Then the mistake will not be regarded as a threat to the director and the latter will be more eager to teach his younger protégé.

People succeed only by making mistakes. Until then a person will not understand the problems of others. Those who do well would benefit from analysing why they did succeed on that occasion; often it was as much a matter of luck as of brains, so be modest about success. Its true nature might also return to haunt you.

The best directors attach great value to goodwill, especially if it is accompanied by gratitude. Both are strong cements. And loyalty, which enables colleagues to go the extra distance, comes by delegating, trusting and almost encouraging staff to make a mistake. The good director will be known to back them in good times and bad, and in a quiet, unostentatious way. Even if often unsuccessful on their behalf, he will have gained their gratitude. In short, there are too many people who gain promotion as a reward for long service instead of for having a go, learning in the process and being reassured by the board that the learning process is acceptable and regarded as constructive.

(There are, though, distinct characteristics to loyalty. First, any enhanced performance will depend largely upon the particular director remaining in position. Second, once he departs there is little likelihood of the benefit being sustained. Third, a firm can lose its loyalty reputation and label if forced to make redundancies. Just as loyalty can help recruitment by making the firm attractive, so redundancies can have the opposite effect. And yet, a lack of loyalty can also benefit recruitment – it can become easier to acquire good people because they no longer have an entrenched wish to remain where they are. So it works both ways. Loyalty can, therefore, and did more so in the past, prevent the market working effectively. Today loyalty to the company is rather temporary, loyalty is now more to one's own career, to oneself!)

Getting people to perform above their ability is one of the most onerous responsibilities of any director, on a par with that of a teacher, but equally rewarding in practice. All too often a company acquires staff from a takeover or merger and somehow, almost magically and instantly, inherits a team of willing personnel, who previously appeared to be just the opposite.

In practice, most "problems" are people problems, and the director needs to recognise this and act quickly. Those around him are actually awaiting careful nurture! However, it is completely inappropriate to merely wait and see how certain underperformers will pan out, whether all will resolve itself and naturally. If the director chooses that route, he needs to acknowledge that he is taking an inordinate risk and will need to inform colleagues that his inaction is planned.

For a director to be popular does not mean that he has to toady for that appreciation. In fact, such people usually fail miserably, creating just the opposite effect on colleagues! And there are few characteristics more exhausting, less sincere and counterproductive than the oversensitive and near sycophantic corporate climber. The popular and successful have different building blocks. They might use humour to make unpalatable points, judging well the nature of the necessary tone, avoiding the downside of appearing frivolous.

Wherever possible, the director will display a sort of neurosis towards customers; this is more likely in a business-to-business situation. It is more difficult to show this when at board level, being more divorced from direct contact with customers, but it will still manifest itself and be detectable to those who bother to look. Customers become loyal, which benefits the bottom line, and colleagues complete the circle by becoming loyal, in turn, to their boss. So the board needs to understand its customer base. If you are a retailer, try stacking shelves on Christmas Eve; it will not take long to know your customers! The director will pick up so much, see a lot and will realise what he is asking his colleagues to put up with.

Successful directors display other, additional characteristics. They understand that there is an inherent opposition to getting a new idea launched. Instead of pushing it through as if the opposition does not exist, however, they try or appear to accommodate their needs, reassuringly, tenaciously and effectively. There is a skill in persuading people that a new idea is their idea or introducing change gradually and quietly.

Getting the best out of people also means not upsetting them. As a director, and particularly as chairman or CEO, remember to treat the annual report with kid gloves when referring to colleagues, especially if by name. By naming only a few, selectively, however relevantly and legitimately, the director might upset others who are not mentioned. It is odd how a chairman can make matters worse in his attempt to make matters better! Incidentally, it is not a bad idea to read the annual report from the back, that is where most of the really interesting data is given.

Ultimately, the success of the company is down to people. Every chairman's annual report acknowledges this (although it is strange how rare it is for the HR director to be on the main board, when so many other functions are and when some are an automatic choice. Is it that the HR function is better represented at board level by another colleague, almost uniquely so? Or is the role not that crucial? Or is every director his own HR director? Perhaps the function has attracted the wrong sort for main board elevation.)

THE DIRECTOR IN THE LOOKING GLASS

Enhancing the performance of those below is one side only of the coin; equally important is for a director to assess his own performance as well. What is motivating him? Is it fear, or greed, or a bit of both, or neither? Is his dream the framework of a vision for all his colleagues, or an unnecessary ego trip to satisfy a closet Napoleon?

A director needs time to think. He needs to be able to do nothing else than that, to walk around his desk a few times before making a decision, but he must not think of everything before acting. All that is asked and required is to make a considered and balanced assessment within the shortest possible time. He is unlike lawyers or academics, for example, who try to take everything into account before coming to their conclusions.

One of the potential advantages of travelling by train is that a director has time to think (even more time when the train is late), separately from the office, colleagues and pressures, cocooned in a world of his own, unknown by his immediate neighbours. What do most directors do in their Arcadia on wheels? They use their mobiles or work on their laptops – behave, in other words, as closely as possible to how they would be behaving if they were still in their offices. Why waste so valuable an advantage? Largely because they have never been taught, or stumbled upon, the advantage of finding time to think.

Moreover, a director needs to be aware that, in general, his young colleagues will be prone to wanting quick solutions, while his older colleagues, and this could include himself, may take the longer view. In between youth and maturity is that rich vein – the younger director who is mature for his age, but who combines youthful energy with probably boundless self-belief.

However, there is no reason why even the older directors should not perform with zest and with a definite spring in their step. Part of the abiding attraction of business is to learn new things, not repeat the same mistakes. To ignore this, to be unaware of the deep satisfaction and stimulation such an outlook generates, means existing in business rather than being absorbed by the process. Business is a reflection of the human condition, a way of developing people, and the individual himself to the full.

At no time, whether in good moments or bad, should the directors regard selfishness as a manifestation of leadership; it quite simply is not. Nor is bullying. The bully merely lives on borrowed time and destroys the ideas of others. Invariably his days will be numbered.

REFOCUSSING

Clearly, most directors will, at sometime in their careers, need to refocus an entire team, not just an individual. It can be an especially valued skill when a company is reaching the second stage of its development, having successfully established itself post-start-up. Rarely, though, will an entire team be at sea. Individuals can be lost and it is up to the chairman or his directors to avoid the one adversely affecting the others. Every team has at least two who actually know what they are doing and those in authority need to harness them in order get the rest to follow.

On any board there will be people who work in unison and a few who might not. The chairman will need to bring the latter into line, getting their strengths to come through. If the whole team actually needs refocussing then shoot a few in order to encourage the rest.

At the initial stage there is a common vision, all rowing together with exuberance into the corporate millpond. All is well, nothing can go wrong. And then it does. Tensions can arise and a storm suddenly whips up this millpond. A refocus can become an urgent priority and the director will need to acknowledge that there is

probably an acute and overriding need urgently to recruit additional skills. It requires self-analysis from the existing directors, the
ability to look at themselves naked in the proverbial mirror. Oddly,
many directors, when asked what they have done to turn their
companies around – apart from the obvious and short-term ones of
cutting the head count or selling divisions – will say, "I've made not
one large, significant decision, but a series of smaller ones." (Some,
possibly most, sources of conflict in corporate life are conflicts of
interest and they only happen when members of the team are
insufficiently honest or open.)

CHANGE AND TRANSITION

If the company is to be sold, either in order to capitalise on success
or as a cruel necessity, the transaction might make the founder
wealthy and perhaps wiser, but it will not compensate for the lack
of purpose and the vacuum in his life. At the time of the transaction,
there is no time for such contemplation; the adrenaline is flowing
fast and furious, the pound-sign is in neon lights and the distinct
prospect of buying independence is all-persuasive and attractive.
Alas, it does not usually turn out to be. (Moreover, the sale can have
unexpected and often detrimental side effects on others as well. It
can produce a psychological shock not only retrospectively for the
founders but for the staff as well, and even for some of their
customers.)

Entrepreneurs live on their nerves, on the next deal, on the buzz
and recognition success gives. From one perspective, being an
entrepreneur today is harder than ever. In the current climate there
is an overriding need to be institutionalised and, when corporate

governance is becoming the vogue, he will, by nature, probably regard that whole movement as nonsense. But while the world appears more hostile to him, he too has characteristics that make his success of either limited duration or effectiveness. Entrepreneurs easily suffer from burn-out. They are merely human beings; they go into decline simply because they are human; they become overconfident, or their company turns into a different type of organisation or, like others, they make a mistake, or a false move, or their luck runs out.

Furthermore, the relationship between the entrepreneur and his staff can change. While he will often generate an inordinate degree of loyalty, it will often be based, in reality, on fear and on the fact that his character appears to be both formidable and larger than life. It is not simply a question of admiration!

Success though can also be sexy – successful people have a certain attraction, however obnoxious the behaviour of some successful people.

No director, whether an entrepreneur, founder director or of a more conventional persuasion, should become beguiled by the skills of others. Never allow yourself to become so under the spell of another that he virtually owns you. It is both farcical and totally unproductive. Nobody, least of all him, will get the best out of you. It is wise to stick to what you know; do not be easily persuaded by others. We are all babes in arms outside our own areas of expertise and it is unwise to stray too far into the corporate territory of others. Some have better presentation skills than others. And, of course, most of us have an unjustifiably low opinion of ourselves, certainly more lowly than is fair or compared with how others see us. Or we ignore the fact that we possess skills that we believe others also possess when they do not.

The scenario is usually most evident when a director joins another board as a non-executive director. Once, when a newly appointed NED was asked how his first board meeting went, he replied that he made one routine, everyday comment and the board said his was the most brilliant, perceptive comment they had ever heard. "But I make such comments every day back at my own company and nobody comments."

Many directors, rather unwisely, have an urge to make statements about the future. Yet such statements, by their nature, are predictions and therefore are judgements; they are not factual. Their successful outcome may depend upon unpredictable factors such as how sales might hold up or how the exchange rate might operate. A director does not have much, if any, control over the second so why prophesy as if he does? Look at any annual report, see both the chairman's and the CEO's statements for the evidence of this routine mistake.

WHEN THE GOING GETS TOUGH

Directors often panic at the first sign of bad news, but that reaction can be totally unjustified. Perhaps the director is newly promoted, and has not previously experienced a period of contraction or consolidation, or a profit that to others is thoroughly healthy but to him a disaster. Even if the news is really bad, the world does not concentrate on one firm or one story for long. Events move on, other stories grab our attention. We flatter ourselves, thinking that our problem is that newsworthy or original. Unfortunately, when a company is doing badly there is a tendency for everybody to look to their own interests, rather like when an empire is disintegrating. It is then that the chairman should play one of his ace cards – to keep the show on the road, in an impartial, selfless manner, putting his own interests second to those of the greater whole.

In business, as in most human endeavour, self-confidence is crucial. Business schools spend a lot of time generating it, some parents pay a lot of money to ensure that it is inculcated into their children and companies rely heavily upon its successful use. But at midnight it can all seem far away, when you are the only person awake apart from politicians and security guards.

Never shoot the messenger as long as his analysis is sound. However rough the feedback, however gloomy the prognosis, the director should seek the truth; otherwise he cannot deal with the problem. When a colleague gives an opinion, however unpalatable, if it is fundamentally sound or challenging, then the director would be very wise to file it in his mind and cross-reference it. Seek counter-arguments both from within and outside the firm and from those – the NEDs – who are uniquely placed in both the internal and external domains. They are the outsiders with an insider feel.

Furthermore, the director should learn to be an effective listener and to ask the right questions. He need not be a trained sleuth, merely a perceptive director. When the right answers have been found, it is important to know how to present them in a way that makes them acceptable. There are those who have not learned the art or necessity of asking a difficult question in a supportive way, avoiding undermining or putting down a colleague on the spot, or being able to say "No" in a positive way.

Although organisations are composed of people, there are occasions when what is appropriate for one is the antithesis for the other. When dealing with people, the director should concentrate on their strengths, not their weaknesses; when dealing with organisations he should concentrate more on what is going wrong, even though this can be especially difficult for a CEO who, by nature, tends to be an optimist.

The director who survives long enough – or who has every intention of doing so rather than taking the remuneration package, facing the music and going – will need to realise that, while companies constantly move up or down, people do not always "move" in unison with the company. The relative speeds are out of kilter, the sway between the organisation, its culture and the majority of the staff is at the wrong inclination. Consequently, there is constant pressure for the director to revitalise the organisation both at the top and at the bottom. Unfortunately, many directors act from the bottom up, or prepare for their "inevitable" parting, especially if they are the CEO. Yet fresh faces, fresh air, renewed curiosity and a degree of courage are all ingredients to be encouraged, to be allowed to filter both up and down the organisation, and thereby revitalise it.

Always be honest, indeed absolutely honest. A half-truth, an exaggeration that is misleading, or any variation on such a theme, is dangerous. The truth nearly always catches up. There is no harm, though, and it is positively beneficial to be enthusiastic and occasionally to appear to be a little over the top. Success or the prospect of it breeds success, and is very intoxicating. Talk up the organisation while trying to ensure that it delivers, but do it with circumspection and care.

Where there are problems, some directors encourage an approach of tackling the smallest ones first. Psychologically, there are advantages and merit in that. It can give incentive to tackle the bigger ones. However, both success and failure are impostors and should be treated the same; even success creates problems, those of complacency. If either is treated wrongly, it can be unnecessarily catastrophic. Surprisingly, companies often meet success and failure too late. (Curiously, many directors linger too long over their mistakes, taking them too much to heart. If they got something wrong once, it does not necessarily mean that the same mistakes will or need be made again. The previous mistake might be a question of lack of clarity and communication, especially towards those below board level – a serious mistake but not one that should produce a reluctance to try again.) In the same vein, it is important for the directors to travel around their group, to see what is happening and thereby not be ambushed. NEDs have a crucial role here, possibly unique, in ensuring that success and failure are treated equally. Advisers should play a part but somehow it seems easier to ignore an adviser, probably believing that one can get away with it. Some will live happily ever after, ignorant of the value of the rejected advice, while others will appreciate its true worth, yet still ignore it, and be effective in disguising their subsequent unease. (There is a growing dichotomy between the company and its professional advisers. Legal advisers in particular are becoming more specialist, at a time when in the main business leaders are becoming more generalist.)

On the whole, directors do not enjoy or endure the top positions in the same company for very long, and the average duration is getting shorter. He might be in his position for less than even the current average of a mere four years. However, interestingly, the rapid turnover of directors can be to their disadvantage rather than a case of letting them go before they do more damage. To regard their settlements enviously in the context of their short tenure may indeed be unjustified, for it is harder than ever to remain in office long enough to succeed.

Perhaps it is partly the director's own fault. He might not have bothered or, at least, failed to take his colleagues with him – to share the vision – but had, instead, succumbed to the culture of sacking those below him before the blade falls on his own neck.

WHO TO TRUST

In fairness, even if he does listen to his colleagues or, worse still, his advisers, the chances are that much of the advice will be wrong. It is not wise to believe all he hears. Perhaps it is better to trust senior colleagues above any adviser, especially if the director works in a smaller firm. In order to achieve the best from the adviser, the director needs to remember two things. He needs to appoint advisers he feels he can trust and he needs to understand how to use them.

It is one of the most confusing conundrums to work out why companies invariably accept the need to pay what can only be regarded as enormous fees to their professional advisers, whether the advice turns out to be useful and correct or not. In the case of audit fees, and the "advice" that accompanies their deliberations at audit committees, it is even less reasonable or desirable. And even less easily explainable if the company is merely a small client of a large general accountancy firm. What is the client really gaining which he would not get by being a big client with a smaller accountancy practice, rather than a small client with a big one? In the former instance, the client is not very important to the professional firm and will, usually, be given a second-best treatment; in the latter the client might actually be worth something. Counter-arguments abound – the gravitas of the bigger firm helps if negotiating a new banking facility, etc. but the best directors do not accept such arguments and subsequent arrangements unchallenged.

It is worthwhile directors adopting the attitude that most consulting on offer is a service that is enjoyable but usually pretty superficial. Their reports can be wayward and the director is entitled to ask if they are retained advisers, why was their retrospective analyses and wisdom not available earlier, i.e. before the horse had bolted? When the Far East dipped in the late 1990s, the articles the next day were perceptive – and would have been of some practical use if they had appeared on the previous day.

Or again, directors should be aware that whereas the best consultants and advisers are very good, possibly world-class, the rest tend to be third-rate. The former are not necessarily the best-known names nor the biggest nor those with the longest track records. And even if the consultancy is the best, especially if it operates in a niche market, there is no guarantee that colleagues will support your advocacy of using them. Many choose on safety grounds, on the long-established assumption that if the best-known is chosen and fails, it is an excusable mistake. Almost hard luck. To make matters worse, consultancy agreements within consultancy firms are of little practical value, either to the firms or to their clients. They simply tend to keep the weaker and allow the better ones to leave. Furthermore, consultants tend to be more proficient at ascertaining what needs to be done rather than the how.

Some companies believe something can be done, regardless of what the market says. Companies often fail to talk to their clients. They choose to believe the consultants.

Frustratingly, a company might appoint a first-division consultancy firm, only to find that instead of getting the "A" team, they get the "C" team within the consultancy. Unfortunately, there is very little the client can do, that time around. Worse still, advisers have their own agendas. Any other rational debate is regarded by them as being silly. Corporate life is littered with examples of deals being pushed through by advisers and consultants who destroy value.

There is a fundamental difference between an adviser/consultant and the client, which is the root cause of much of the subsequent mutual disillusionment; it is the difference between those who understand how the business works and those who analyse it. Businesses have cultures, analysts ignore this.

Unfortunately, few advisers urge their clients to be as bold as they sometimes ought or need be. If a director should cut overheads – and that is often the first and obvious item on the panic list – they will chip away at the problem, cutting perhaps 10 per cent rather than the necessary 20 per cent. The director will argue that it can be 10 per cent now, and if more is needed later, he can advocate a further 10 per cent. However, it is best to make the full 20 per cent now, thus avoiding two disruptions and two painful steps.

It is very unwise for a director, however successful, to compare his performance or that of his company with internally set yardsticks. The competition does not stand still. If his company is a clear market leader he does have one considerable advantage over those trailing behind. It costs a disproportionate amount of money and time to catch a market leader. Meanwhile, the successful company could well be subject to a high degree of criticism from both the press and from the market, if for no other reason than because the company is the market leader, the one to beat.

Directors should learn or remember to be diplomatic and circumspect. Careless talk can kill a deal, prevent a promotion and demoralise staff. Chairs have ears and know other chairs. The coincidences are so frequent and relevant that they are almost improbable; certainly they would not appear legitimate in a work of fiction. Whether in airport departure lounges, on planes, in trains, in restaurants or at private functions be diplomatic, circumspect and sensible.

In addition, there is a need for directors to keep their feet on the ground and remain modest especially vis-à-vis their friends. Sometimes the director changes, forgetting that he can also slip down the ladder – and easier and quicker than he ascended it. Surprisingly, perhaps, it is often the spouses who change most when the husband succeeds. They become cocky and self-important; a corporate night at Covent Garden, the best box, all expenses paid, function after function. The only known way of retrieving a friendship in such circumstances is for the director to lose his job. Then, almost overnight, the wife reverts back to her nicer ways.

It is a sad sight when the director is discarded, is put out to pasture, especially when involuntarily or before he has made the necessary psychological adjustments. He can become frustrated; activities that meant a lot when squeezed into a busy weekend lose their appeal and meaning. Visits to galleries, the enjoyment of being able to shop in the best places, the chance of more holidays – all lose their shine rather rapidly. Indeed, there are restaurants and galleries, shops and theatres awash with former directors who have been forced off the business stage prematurely – age-wise – and are desperate to be wanted and to work in a proper, demanding job again – a sentiment also shared by their wives!

Or again, some companies might appear to the outsider to be well run and to be performing well, but the reality could be very different. Images are often based on the average performance of others in their sector, and that generally could be poor.

Interestingly, directors need to be more aware of how to deal with another external factor and yet are invariably ill-prepared to do so. The press are a mixed blessing to any director. Officially most, but by no means all, seek their attention and then regret their interpretation of events or assessment of the company's character. In most cases, the press give an incomplete picture and only apologise if there is a threat of being sued. Sometimes, journalists' behaviour makes companies conclude, probably erroneously, that they are either stupid or careless or, alas, in some cases both. It is often better to spend money attempting to avoid getting a mention in the press, or in at least asking their photographers at results time not to take photographs, usually of the CEO and finance director looking especially silly, against a jokey, asinine background. What is particularly galling about the press is that if they get something wrong – and they do often – the original, incorrect story appears on page one whereas the apology, if given, and usually reluctantly, can appear around page six.

In fairness to the press, directors become paranoid about the press, especially when their company is doing badly and that means usually when it is in decline. Hence, it is safer not to have a high profile even though that might be contrary to what the burgeoning, corporate-PR, investor-relations industry advocates. Instead, the company should take trouble with their own investors and with the presentation of their results and, where possible, consolidate that relationship on a personal basis.

SEARCHING FOR A WIDER ROLE

There are some directors who reach a stage when they feel that they want to strut a wider stage; they look at their own representative body, trade association or council or, perhaps one of the umbrella organisations, such as the CBI, IOD and the EEF. It is entirely legitimate to want to "put something back" (as many directors say) but it is sometimes better to become public-spirited or self-interested at the official end of an active career. Otherwise, it is easy for that career to end prematurely.

Representative bodies need voluntary and relevant input, new faces and some bright outsiders offering enthusiasm. But many directors spend too much time in such bodies, take their eyes off the ball back at their own companies and pay, along with their shareholders, a heavy corporate price for so doing. It also then reflects badly on such bodies themselves, discrediting their message or making them obvious fodder for an unkind press.

Incidentally, if the director seeks an external appointment, with pay, and via the appointments board of the Cabinet Office, expect at least one of three things to happen. The selection process will prove inordinately long; the remit will turn out to be unreasonably large; and the financial reward minuscule, even accepting, rightly, that those seeking public office should sacrifice some remuneration for the "honour".

Successful business people are used to speedy selection processes. Whitehall is not. It is a question of two cultures made worse by Whitehall believing that it has adopted private sector methods and adapted them for its own needs. In practice, this is hardly the case. There is a need for the process to be thorough and thoroughly transparent, to encourage as wide a group of potential candidates as possible; even, perhaps – although surely the jury is out – representative of all vested interests. (Whitehall could learn from the private sector here; the best boards are the smallest, the least "representative" in Whitehall parlance, but with the right chemistry.)

Despite these apparent endless potential pitfalls, and the likelihood that tenure at the top will be all too brief, there is still no in-built, inevitable reason for a director's career to end so frequently in failure. The basic premise that business is a simple exercise made unnecessarily complicated, albeit with a thin line between success and failure, still holds true.

INDEX